MISSION TO THE POOREST

By M. R. Loew, O.P.

Translated by Pamela Carswell

With an Introduction and Epilogue by Maisie Ward

This is a companion volume to *France Pagan?*, constructed on the same model—in the centre the translation of a book by a French priest working among the proletariat, preceded by a sketch of the priest who wrote it, followed by an account of developments since.

Though constructed on the same model it is a very different book, equally necessary to those who would follow one of the most remarkable priestly movements in the world. Père Loew, the author, is a Dominican: two things make his work especially important—he conducts his proletarian mission as a parish priest, and he is a trained sociologist.

His book tells of his own work, and that of the laymen he enlisted, in the dock-area of Marseilles: how he became a docker and a slum-dweller. There can hardly be anywhere a more vivid account of the realities of life in a slum. The epilogue by Maisie Ward tells of the present situation: he has a community of four priests—two Dominicans, a Jesuit, and a secular—living together, two going out to work to support all four, living as their parishioners live.

A main delight of the book is Père Loew, no wild-eyed idealist, but the coolest realist that ever sacrificed himself totally for an ideal.

MISSION TO THE POOREST

MISSION TO THE POOREST

BY

M. R. LOEW

With an Introduction and Epilogue
BY
MAISIE WARD

Foreword by
ARCHBISHOP CUSHING

SHEED AND WARD
LONDON
1950

FIRST PUBLISHED 1950
BY SHEED AND WARD, LTD.
110/111 FLEET STREET,
LONDON, E.C.4

This book is a translation
by
PAMELA CARSWELL

of *En Mission Prolétarienne*, by Père Loew.

PRINTED IN GREAT BRITAIN
BY PURNELL AND SONS, LTD.
PAULTON (SOMERSET) AND LONDON

FOREWORD

SOMETHING of the hidden wonder of the repetition in the life of the Church of all the joyful, sorrowful and glorious mysteries of the life of Christ is exemplified in the story of modern France.

Who could possibly understand why France is still "the eldest daughter of the Church" when he reads of the widespread "de-Christianization" of that land? Yet who would have recognized the Son of God in the broken, bleeding man who dragged the Cross to Calvary?

Who would expect to see a springlike revival of the Faith in the very midst of the disillusioned masses of the French proletariat? Yet who would have looked for Easter at the cold, silent door of the Tomb that Good Friday night two thousand years ago?

To sustain their Faith through Good Friday and Holy Saturday the Apostles had the promises of Christ. The Church has His promises still: *Behold, I am with you all days even to the consummation of the world.*

And so, when the powerful, the privileged and the high-placed forget God or fail to fulfil their complete responsibility to Him, Catholicism continues undaunted her "mission to the poorest", that out of their salvation she may reap her richest spiritual harvest in these dark days.

Such was the mission of Père Loew, whose story Pamela Carswell and Maisie Ward have brought us in this truly moving translation of an inspiring chapter in modern religious history. It illustrates in terms of the apostolic work of one man in contemporary France the perennial power of

v

the Gospel to renew the hearts of men and to change the face of the earth.

Catholics scandalized by social trends, fearful of what the future may bring, will be refreshed by the story of this Catholic sociologist of a most practical kind. They will be indebted to Sheed and Ward for making it available to us.

✝RICHARD J. CUSHING
Archbishop of Boston

Archbishop's House
Brighton, Mass.

CONTENTS

Père Loew—Catholic Sociologist

MAISIE WARD

A LARGE group of Frenchmen in touch with the present revival of their Church, asked to name the most important books concerning that revival, put *En Mission Proletarienne*, here translated by Pamela Carswell under the title *Mission to the Poorest*, at the very head of their list. Abbé Godin answered his own challenge in *France Pays de Mission* by establishing the Mission de Paris. Père Loew has gone rapidly forward, writing in the *Mission de Marseille* an authentic new page in the historical development that we are witnessing today.

As history in general, it may be summarised in the famous saying "The Church begins again". The Church of France, whose fortunes appeared linked to those of the old regime, which had lost or never possessed the populace of the new great cities and had hung about the countryside ever less and less in touch with the new generations, that Church has raised its head and entered on a fresh life of conquest and achievement. Pius XI lamented that in the nineteenth century the working class had been lost to the Church. Hence it was natural enough that the emphasis of Catholic Action started under him should be laid emphatically upon that class. As one studies it more closely one realises that in fact it embraces closely all strata of French life. But the approach to the workers is at once the newest, the most adventurous and the most exciting. It is far too soon to sum up its results, but each priest who has entered upon this special apostolate has something special to tell us about it. Père Loew writes of his own contribution:

"The title of this book is meant to indicate both its spirit and content: the story of a missionary apostolate aiming at the evangelisation of the proletariat, and attempting to provide an adequate and effective answer to the various needs and obstacles which it has encountered.

"But it is an interim account only, so there is nothing final, nothing dogmatic about it: a simple, sometimes repetitious, day-to-day record, a letter and a brotherly greeting addressed to all those who, at Paris, Colombes, Lisieux, Lyons or elsewhere, are pioneering the same road.

"Many are more advanced, and truly this is cause for joy, but they themselves will rejoice to know that others are clearing and marking out paths which converge on their own."

There are two things which seem to make this book more important than the author realises. For he is both the first priest to unite a proletarian mission with a parish and the first sociologist to have created a mission and parish. A visit to Marseilles convinced me of the quite primary importance of what is being done there.

It was a little difficult to decide on the best method of presenting this significant book and its still more significant author. On reflexion I have thought it best to begin by an introductory chapter on his work as a sociologist—for out of this grew all the rest. Next come the seven chapters in which Père Loew records the story of his missionary work up to the time of his taking over a parish. Chapter VIII, "After Three Years", forms no part of the French edition of the book. Written after three years' parochial experience, as a report to his bishop, it represents above all the deepening under-standing of the problem that this experience brought. Naturally enough nothing is said in it of the result of the experiment as seen from outside. The electric effect upon an observer of witnessing the parish life, even briefly, has made me feel it worth while to add an epilogue on Père Loew as Parish Priest. The profound unity revealed under these various aspects will, I hope, emerge throughout the book. Parts of the French introductions and appendices are out of date. The remainder I have broken up so as to fit them in where they best belong in this volume which aims at depicting the man as well as his share in a great movement.

Must Catholics in the social field, asks Monsignor Ancel (in *Témoignage Chrétien*), always be trying to ally themselves with an outworn Capitalism on the one hand, or with a Communism which they vainly hope to purge of its atheist materialism on the other? Cannot they create something fresh?

But, most Catholics would reply, we are so few. We cannot hope to impose our ideas on the masses of our fellow citizens: we *must* ally ourselves with some larger group.

In the light of history this hardly seems a valid argument. The early Christians were few, the early Communists appeared inconsiderable: creative thought carries with it first the little band of real thinkers and enthusiasts, and presently the masses. Surely our trouble is not so much that we are few as that we are doing too little creative thinking. In no field can it be said more truly than in the sociological that Catholics, however good their wills, have minds just like the rest of the world's—apart from some Catholic patches.[1]

I remember as a child hearing an old cousin scolding my mother for praying for temporal benefits and asserting that she herself never did so. Then in a sudden access of honesty

[1] F. J. Sheed in a lecture on "The Catholic Mind".

she added in an aside, "except of course my investments". There was a storm of laughter. The farmer must not pray for rain or the schoolboy for a fine day, but old Theresa could pray for her investments. Did she ever remember her name-saint whose Book of Foundations would be a useful manual for Catholic sociologists? But no, for Saint Theresa belonged to one department of life and the investments to another. It is not fair to say of these people that they took their religion out with their best dresses on Sundays only. They used it every day to go to Mass, to meditate, to give alms, to be kind to those around them. Only it was not brought to bear on the social order. Investments were something that produced an income: one did not ask whether they flowed from houses too highly rented or from factories that were sweat shops, but one did most conscientiously set aside a proportion of that income for charity.

Today I fancy that though that same old cousin might still be praying for her investments, she might equally well be what has been called an "encyclical Catholic"—one who talks much of the need for social reform but does not fail to enjoy what she possesses until that reform catches up with her. For the social pendulum of the Western world has swung, and many Catholics are swinging with it. The nineteenth century exalted Capitalism—but also charity. The twentieth century decries Capitalism but is highly dubious of the value of charity.

Père Loew, like Abbé Godin, insists steadily on the Catholic's double duty: of acting as a Catholic here and now among his fellows, and of working unceasingly towards "*réformes de structure*". But he has done something more. He has himself entered the field of sociology as an expert, so as to command the attention of other experts, in a small but pregnant book, *Les Dockers de Marseille*.

Production, distribution, consumption, currency: the reduction of the science of political economy to these abstractions will appear to our descendants, thinks Père Loew, absolute childishness—or worse. Worse, because in the true childhood of the science economists handled conditions with far more actuality. Today, like an adolescent at his most ungraceful age, they scorn what was best in their early efforts. Modern techniques might indeed improve on the occasional inaccuracy of their first approaches, but it is sheer loss to confuse these techniques with an ever increasing departmentalising and narrowness of outlook.

Economists of the Gide school, attempting a reaction against this narrowness, have declared "The consumer is all in all". But no, says Père Loew, "it would be more accurate to say the opposite, for the greatness of man lies more in creating than in consuming. Once again, the only solution . . . consists in dealing with man in his concrete reality, complex indeed but living. This is a much harder task, demanding infinitely greater labour and patient submission to reality. But it enables one to go ahead on sure ground even if only step by step".

It was with this ideal in mind that *Economie et Humanisme* was brought into existence in 1942.

The excessive departmentalising of which Père Loew complains largely arose from the fact that economists and sociologists alike conducted their studies in libraries and announced their findings from platforms: men and conditions were no more than abstractions for their consideration. Père Lebret, founder of *Economie et Humanisme*, deplored the prevalence of this attitude even among Catholic sociologists: they were, he said, too abstract. From 1930 to 1939 he had been working at St. Malo among the deep-sea fishermen. Finding them defenceless against ship-owners, local markets and various types of exploitation, he had studied the national and international marketing situation and the principles whereby a better set-up might be achieved. His work is reminiscent of that of Fathers Tomkins and Coady at Antigonish, Nova Scotia. "He regretted", writes Fr. Serrand, "that the *Semaines Sociales* confined themselves too exclusively to theories and generalities. His desire was to create organisms in accord at once with the Church's social teaching and with the concrete needs of the moment. In 1940–1, in view of the disordered state of France, he joined forces with some economists, business managers and working men, thus widening his first conception. From this group, dominated by the powerful personality of Père Lebret, *Economie et Humanisme* was born". *Les Dockers de Marseille* and *Mission to the Poorest* are typical of its publications, which are mainly documentary. First established at Marseilles, its offices are now in Paris.

It is not so much, Père Loew considers, a question of "linking" social with economic as of recognising their already existent "vital interpenetration". "The economic and the social have always been one thing—for the good of all men through many centuries, for their misfortune during the last eighty years".

This period of eighty years[1] may appear, especially to the English reader, somewhat arbitrarily chosen—and about a hundred years too late—but it here has reference to the specialised study that forms the subject of *Les Dockers de Marseille*, the genesis of which is briefly referred to on the first page of *Mission to the Poorest*. For, told by his superiors to study "fats and oils", he quickly turned from books to people. Nor was this from lack of skill in handling written material. *Les Dockers de Marseille* is quite exceptionally able

[1] Now nearer ninety: the book was written in 1942.

in its assembling of facts and figures: the analyses of races and languages, of the numbers of dockers actually employed as against the artificial figures given on lists; the maps and plans that show at a glance what living conditions are in an average slum area—all this is most admirably done.

Then, too, Père Loew was a lawyer before he became a priest, and he moves with ease among the complicated legal discussions and decisions which alone can make clear the story of the catastrophe which now nearer ninety than eighty years ago overtook the city. But the most important thing about this book of facts is that we see through the facts living men and women.

If you go up to Notre Dame de la Garde by means of the *Ascenseur*, you have an amazing impression of rising over the beautiful old red roofs into the sky. Not even in an aeroplane have I ever felt the world so quickly dropping beneath my feet. And when, after visiting Our Lady in her rather ugly shrine—but you feel she must indeed have wanted to dwell in it, that the glorious beauty of mountains, hills and sea should lift men's minds to God—you drop down the hill again, you find yourself at the doors of a soap factory. Like the red roofs, the soap factory makes a brave show for the visitor. Here are tempting little boxes of expensive tablets, each one with its appropriate flower glowing on the wrapper —rose, violet, jasmine. And there is *Entrée libre*: you can go in and see how the soap is made. And when you have seen it you will know less than Père Loew after his week's dispiriting study of text-books. For *to understand conditions you must get right into them.*

The heart of the real Marseilles is the docks: it is a babel of languages: Frenchmen, Italians, Greeks, Spaniards, Turks, Maltese, Africans, Russians, all rub shoulders there, are all part of its vast army of casual labour, live many of them in

national communities herded together in one of the neighbouring slums. So it was into the docks, as he tells us below,
that Père Loew decided to go as a workman. In both books
he makes intensely vivid the sufferings he thus shared: the
uncertainty of employment and hence of food and lodging,
the heavy, dirty nature of most of the work, the endless
waiting in queues—often to find as you reach the head of the
line the door banging in your face: closing hour has come.
The endless complications of forms to fill, the utter carelessness of the men's time, the taking on at busy periods of
more "hands" than the port can carry: the awful anonymity, so that men may work for years and make no human
contact with their employers. Then, too, they must live near
the docks to save time and tram tickets: they must get up at
five for the hope of employment, wait at the *bistro* for an hour
for work to start if they have been taken on, for five hours if
they have failed to get a job in the morning and want to try
again in the afternoon. No money to take the tram home,
very little chance to wash off grime and coal dust: even their
fellow workmen tend to despise and avoid the dockers, who
have become a sub-proletariat—casual, unorganised, half-
starved, unwashed men. And if Père Loew feels all this
through living in it and enduring it, he is still more keenly
conscious of what it means from the historical studies he was
pursuing in the intervals of his physical labours. For the
dockers are the lineal descendants of the *portefaix* who were
an aristocracy of labour in Marseilles right down to the early
1860s. A trades union? A friendly society? Both these things,
but indeed much more like a medieval guild—and this
naturally enough, for the first mention of them occurs before
the end of the fourteenth century.

The book of rules drawn up in 1817 consisted of four parts,
twenty-one chapters, three hundred and ten articles designed

to "protect each man's rights and preserve the union and harmony that should reign in our society".

Into this highly honoured fraternity entry cost the stranger a thousand francs in the money of 1817 (for a short while even one thousand five hundred); for the son of a member it cost only eight francs. The gulf was deliberate. Membership ran in families: there were whole generations of *portefaix*. An immensely high standard of honour, probity and quality of work was enforced by the officers: in return merchants entrusted to the foremen the keys of their warehouses, left to them the checking of their goods and trusted them absolutely to see that nothing was damaged in delivery.

Five doctors were employed by the society for its members: sick and accident benefits were assured them, hospitalisation in case of need, and old age pensions. Before admission the five doctors had to examine the candidate and give him a health certificate. He must be between twelve and forty years of age, a qualified worker and of good life and behaviour. To all this was added a six months' *noviciat* before admission to full membership.

The entry fees, fines for misdemeanours, and a three per cent levy on the total receipts, provided sufficient funds for the running expenses and for the social benefits. For men living far from the port additional local doctors were employed, and the rule for the salaries was quite simply that each should receive an equal part of the total payment earned by their joint work. The men worked in teams; the numbers were not allowed to grow bigger than the port could carry. To ensure this, the society had in fact a monopoly in the work of loading and unloading ships—and this monopoly formed the excuse for its undoing.

Between 1861 and 1863 new docks were being built, and a new society had come into being—the *Compagnie des Docks*.

Established in the first instance to build shops and ware-houses in the vicinity, they were soon claiming the right to engage their own labour for loading and unloading, putting forward the thesis of free competition so acceptable to nine-teenth century Liberalism, and claiming the rights (no less undisputed) that went with the property that they had con-tracted to create—and had created.

"To take from the Dock [Company] the exclusive right of handling the goods lodged in its warehouses is to take away from it the greater part of its legitimate reward; it is clearly a breach of the contract of concession."[1]

This thesis is qualified by Père Loew as *summum jus, summa injuria*. It appeared so manifestly reasonable, and the case was completed by the claim that the work could be better, more cheaply and more swiftly done *for the service of the public* by the dock company than by the antiquated society of the *portefaix* who were chiefly concerned with the wellbeing of their own members.

Using language as skilfully as he carried loads it was a *portefaix* foreman who answered in words so prophetic that it took only a few years to witness their realisation. You are, he told the company, saying in fact: "All these men are earning a good living: let us embezzle their business and we can pile up their profits in our bank. It is true that by sub-stituting the hireling for the free workman, the day labourer for the man with a contract, we shall reduce many families to ruin. The general level of morality will be lowered, the sense of personal dignity will be weakened together with that of responsibility: commerce will no longer be served by trust-worthy men devoted to its interests, but by hostile or at best indifferent hirelings—but what matter? Our shareholders will grow rich, and when we have created destitution we shall

---

[1] *Les Portefaix et le Dock* quoted in *Les Dockers de Marseille*, p. 37.

christen it progress and administrative ability" (*haute administration*).

In vain did the ancient society of *portefaix* attempt to fight back against the wealth of the new company—indeed also against the current of thought that supported the "liberal" thesis of the day. Many men no doubt thought that the *portefaix* had carried matters with a high hand around the docks; many, that their restriction of employment was an evil. Anyhow, the law saw freedom otherwise than did the *portefaix*. Attempts on their part to continue to restrict the workers within their old limits, to regulate the work by its old laws, were legally defeated—and within a few decades the prosperous *portefaix* had turned into the starving docker.

Only one comfort can be drawn from this sorry story: the very speed of the metamorphosis points to the fact that social change need not of necessity be a work of centuries. True, it is easier to destroy than to create, yet Père Loew's book has already done something. He is working towards a much greater thing—a real reform in the structure of the dock economy, bringing it closer to its old shape. But meanwhile the book has caused quite a stir, and by the time it went into a second edition it had already borne some fruit.

The German occupation halted all activity at the docks for three years, and this perhaps gave time for facts and ideas to sink in. Anyhow, workmen's syndicates, technicians and masters all agreed that measures of decasualisation for the dockers must somehow be applied. The result has been the institution of a "guaranteed salary". No longer at least does a docker return home empty-handed on a day when no ship is there to be unloaded. He is paid a poor wage (usually four hundred francs), but he is paid a wage. He can buy food for the day if he is a single man eating at a *bistro*. He can take home a little to lighten the burden of housekeeping if he has a wife and family. And not only does this apply in Marseilles; a *caisse nationale* has been established for all the dockers of France. The extremity of hazard in their lives is eased. Perhaps some day it will be lifted.

A final chapter was added to the second edition of *Les Dockers de Marseille* in 1945—before even this minor but very real reform had taken place. In it Père Loew states the three fixed points around which any real reform must be built.

1. Limitation and freezing of the numbers of dockers employed.
2. Obligation of these "professional" dockers to supply the necessary work.
3. Certainty for them that work will always be available.

In this chapter we are given also an entirely new picture— the docks in the hands of the American Army. For after the Liberation came a time of immense prosperity for the docker. The work periods were changed to ten-hourly engagements; "boys, old men, the lame, the fit and the unfit had only to offer themselves and they were taken on".

We can see Père Loew watching the scene, fascinated by the American soldiers with their novel habits, rejoicing at first over the prosperity for his old friends—and then sad- dened as he meditated over a new species of unemployment no less disastrous than the old.

"Nothing demoralises men more totally than to be paid to do nothing. In a quiet place with their minds at rest they might simply dream out their paid holidays. But here amid din of engines and clouds of dust the idle man must quickly learn the art of appearing to be busy.

"What is he likely to get busy about? Probably the best way of stealing something out of the most valuable pack- ages. What will be his chief topic of conversation—usually

the lowest and filthiest things he can think up on a subject
that it would be a profanation to call by the name of love.

"Or ten hours of hanging about are spent in gambling
openly on the dock—one man may lose in a single night
the ten thousand francs entrusted to him by his wife to be
put in the Savings Bank. Sometimes I have seen the
stakes in this open-air casino go as high as fifty to eighty
thousand francs."

Many of the men felt the evil themselves. "It will take
twenty years to turn back the stream" one young worker
said. "The reform of the port", continues Père Loew,
"must be accompanied by a great effort at education of the
workers." They must regain "their honour as workmen,
their professional conscience. But education will be useless
and the stream will never be turned back except in a port
organised for the men and by the men who work there: the
old insecurity renewed every half-day, the ten-hour periods
spent without raising a finger, are equally inhuman.

"A private enterprise that unjustly withholds the wages
due to the worker cries out for the vengeance of heaven, but
a huge state organisation in which a man's least movements
are directed by a remote office is equally horrifying . . .

"The re-discovery of man. This study began with man
and with man it must be ended. At the port, in his daily
work on the quays, light must be sought on the solutions to
be chosen and on those to be rejected."

In his determination to go ahead step by step on ground
thoroughly surveyed, Père Loew's analysis of his chosen
narrow territory is akin to Christopher Dawson's far wider
yet equally detailed vision. Neither man can be faulted by
the experts who reject the insight of a Chesterton or a Vincent
McNab because of their inaccuracies. This carelessness was
certainly a misfortune: the insight was there, the deep in-

tuitions of reality, but far less effectively for the world that needed them.

But the main importance of Père Loew's work lies in its appeal from a narrow departmentalism to the fullness of man's reality. This is the field in which Catholic sociology is beginning to find itself. It is through the discovery of "Man the Forgotten" that its bases are being most surely laid.

Thus Chesterton in *What's Wrong With the World* went straight to the fundamental questions—what is sex, wherein is woman really different from man, what effect should this have on the education of boys and girls? And again, what are man's fundamental needs: the family; a home; property. What effect does this have on the shaping of society? And who can forget those other words of Chesterton's uttered before the war had made them so poignant, that we shall only deal rightly with the refugee problem when we see each family of fugitives as the Holy Family fleeing before Herod's soldiers?

Thus, too, Borne and Henry, in their valuable study of the Philosophy of Work, bringing back the medieval conception of work's redemptive value, analyse in it also the fulfilment of man's nature as a creative and a social being. Meeting what is best in Communism with their affirmations of work's goodness they show the inevitable failure of Communism from not seeing all action as leading to Contemplation. Man, Newman once said, is not only a thinking animal—he is a feeling, acting, contemplating animal. Catholic thinkers who insist on looking at man in his fullness are in fact beginning to "create something fresh".

And it is noteworthy that in this creation men draw together who would certainly find themselves in opposite political camps if they had merely to choose from the parties that surround them.

The preface to *Les Dockers de Marseille* is written by Gustave Thibon, a man so traditionalist in his thinking that I once heard an enraged young Catholic exclaim, "Why, this is nothing but:

"God bless the squire and his relations
And keep us all in our proper stations."

Yet Père Loew himself has often been called a Communist. In actual fact he is rather like Belloc's young man who was disinherited by his aunt for socialism on account of "a lecture he had delivered against that economic theory".

Catholics who are clear about fundamental principles can work together to an amazing degree on their application. Catholics who are muddled are constantly excommunicating one another.

It is from Thibon that Père Loew takes an analogy which helps him to clarify what exactly the men and women of a mission are attempting in establishing themselves in a pagan proletarian area.

"To save a drowning man you must throw yourself into the water with him, but you must be a better swimmer. There must be always *Communauté de Destin*.

"This analogy enables us to solve the problem of an élite. To throw yourself into the water means to share the same life, the same difficulties, the same risks, to join your life to the man you want to save. *But* you must be a better swimmer: that means you must have within you resources that the drowning man lacks: courage, energy, a clear view of the facts and of the ways of bringing off the rescue. You must have taken, before plunging in, the necessary deep breath. You must not presume on your own strength—for you have studied its limitations. You must, in short, be constantly preoccupied with assembling within yourself everything that may be useful when the moment comes. None of this separates you from the

drowning man. It is not because they swim badly that
certain swimming-teachers do so little life-saving, but
because they are afraid of throwing themselves into the
water".

This quotation is taken from Appendix III—tucked away
at the back of the French edition of *Mission to the Poorest*.

In the book the story is told of the beginnings of a Residence of women as part of the Mission: in the Appendix its
possibilities are discussed. But the ideas in this apparently
unimportant Appendix are so capital to an understanding of
Père Loew as sociologist that it seems better to discuss them
here.

The "Settlement" was, as he tells us, an English nineteenth century idea, and the Residence is its legitimate
development—benefiting by the changes of time and the
progress of ideas. For while the Settlement was made up
entirely of well-to-do people coming into a poor area to do
it service, the Residence must draw together girls of all
classes, among whom those who do not already belong to
the area must be *naturalised*. Everything they do must be
done, not by the Residence but by the *Quartier*. They must
become an intimate part of its life, its very heart. There
should ideally be a mixture of bourgeoises and working girls.
Some should go out to factories to earn money for the support
of the house, others stay at home to housekeep, nurse the
sick and be simply neighbourly.

These girls should live in the style and rhythm of the area
—neither poorer nor richer than the average. Here at once,
I was told by a very striking young woman whose work is
chiefly among the sick and destitute, arises a surprising sort
of difficulty. The idea of living in poverty and of working
in a factory has an immense attraction for many girls—the

type who in an earlier generation would have entered con-
vents. But they are apt to look on it too much from the angle
of self-sacrifice and of personal sanctification. All want to
go to the factory: but if all go to the factory the balance is
lost: neighbourliness, visiting, care of the sick are at a dis-
count. Then, too, these same girls want to be *too* poor.
How, asked this fascinating flaming little Marseillaise, can
we teach good management unless we keep the same
resources as our neighbours, how can we make a welcoming
atmosphere if no one is at home to welcome them?

No, says Père Loew, the Mission, the Residence, are not
an invitation to poverty in a spirit of direct penance, as an
aid to contemplation, or even to set an example of evangelical perfection. They have one object: to direct energy
and intelligence towards the abolition of a definite social
evil. A Resident has plunged into the water to save the
drowning man. And if one danger lies in drifting apart from
him, there is, too, the other danger of letting him drag you
under. Père Loew is careful to point out the requisites that
make of a Residence a real instrument of salvation even in
the daily details of a shared existence. He spends a page on
the simplicity yet elegance that should mark the room where
visitors are welcomed. Never receive from behind a desk:
the official note spoils everything. Not in the kitchen: that
is friendly but no conversation is possible. There should be
a special room, light, bright, with armchairs and flowers:
a "cosy corner such as you find in an American bar" is the
perfect place for a relaxed talk. Children must be kept out
of this favoured spot, and boys and girls only admitted if they
can behave nicely. And the Resident herself? "The ideal
would be for her to unite all the qualities of a perfect young
society hostess with the friendliness of the girl at the counter
of a popular bar who sets you instantly at ease."

The Residence is to be the "drawing-room" of the *Quartier*. It must set an example of what is possible even in poverty: never must the Residence sink to being a slum within a slum. "Cleanliness is the dignity of the poor: personal cleanliness, clean clothes, a clean house: there must be no hesitation, no discussion on this point." Its aim, like that of the Mission as a whole, is "to make men, and to help men to live like men". To attain this end real thought is needed —and particularly this thought must be concerned with the "dignity of the poor man". Père Loew uses the expression again and again. The Residents must be helpful as neighbour to neighbour: but not allow themselves to be "milked like a cow"—less for their own sakes than because to allow this is in fact to lower the dignity of the worker. And one of the chief benefits that they can bring to him is a realisation of that dignity.

Père Loew has seen that dignity outraged: he has seen it forgotten: he is labouring to help the workers in their efforts to restore it.

"The Residence is not a game or a record of visits, of advice, of surgical dressings and of injections. Love and physical strength are not enough to give, without *the effort of the mind*. The Residence is not there merely to fight day by day against the physical and moral sufferings of an area. It is there to take part in the great movements of man's civilisation, especially the *mouvement ouvrier*."

The very sensitivity that has made of Père Loew a sociologist who realises his own share in the humanity he is dissecting, very nearly lost this book for us altogether. Had he the right to tell this story of the sorrows and the tragedies of others: to unveil their secrets to an indifferent world? He describes the protest made to him by a companion in the apostolate:

"Tell me quite honestly—if, on your way, you had recognised your mother or your sister, would you have offered her to the curious gaze of the public? Would you have found it in you to publish her name, this woman or child that we have both tried to help?

"I do not believe that you have the right to violate the secrets of their lives, of their physical, moral, social wretchedness. They are not curiosities, the subjects of an experiment, something to be exposed in show-cases or popular magazines.

"Father, you have never wept with hunger, and seen your dear ones weep with hunger. You have never known what it is like to be *really* out of work, to hear someone say, 'Give me your name, you will be notified . . .'

"I entreat you, respect the secrets of others, do not disclose things which are not yours to tell."

With Père Loew's own answer this introduction may well conclude. For it is indeed a reminder to us all that to the Catholic there can be no such thing as a purely academic sociology. Whether we will it or not we have with all men a *communauté de destin*—the common lot, not only of one humanity, one red clay of which the first man was fashioned— but also the common lot of membership in the new and redeemed humanity of Christ.

Père Loew then answers his friend:

"One hesitates long after such burning words. Silence, is not this the safest course? There are decencies more compelling, a nakedness more distressing, than those of the body.

"And yet, how is one to act effectively, to avoid betray-ing the truth, if one does not enlighten those who are unaware of what actually, genuinely takes place barely a few hundred yards from where they live? How, without shouting at the top of one's voice, can one prevent the distance widening, the gulf deepening every day between

those who could act—who must act—but who are unconscious of the situation, and those who can no longer do
anything . . .?

"This is no matter of trying to touch people's feelings,
appealing to their compassion; rather is it one of crying
out before it is too late, before the day when we shall
hear it from His own lips, the words of Christ: 'As long
as you did it not to one of the least of these . . .'

"We should be but part-witnesses of Christ if we bore
witness to Jesus of Nazareth only; we have also to pro-
claim the sufferings of the Body of Christ as it exists at
the present time, as we encounter it every day in our
cities, wandering and vagrant, lacking shelter, lacking air
and light and warmth, alone in the world without work,
without hope and without God.

"This, then, is the sole justification for speaking.

"Your secret, my destitute brothers, my companions
whom I love and respect with all that is best in me, does
not belong to yourselves alone. It is that of the Saviour,
just as your body is not yours alone, but His too. And we
all communicate in this same Body—we too, although
after you. In short, we are but One. And since, again,
the remedy for our ills is not found in chemists' shops or
laboratories but consists in changing the 'social pressure',[1]
it is imperative that all co-operate in the immense effort
of recovery.

"Millions of men have fallen to the bottom of the abyss,
and who can flatter himself that he is far from the edge?
This book, among so many others, sends out an appeal to
all Christians of good will for a gigantic heave at the
rescue-line—gigantic, yes, and yet in practice it is so
simple: for all one has to do is to take one's place at the
rope."

[1] Mgr. Saliège.

PART ONE

CHAPTER I

Donning Overalls

July–December, 1941.

"FATHER LOEW, you will be studying fats and oils." These words of Father Lebret, my new superior, send a faint chill through me. I have just emerged from the seminary after seven years' study, and I certainly didn't become a Dominican in order to devote myself to peanuts and soap.

Submissively, I say to myself, "Oh, well, fats and oils it is!" I visit a factory, take away a stout treatise on the manufacture of soap, nearly buy a little book on chemistry but decide that it is too complicated, and take an elementary school textbook instead.

At the end of a week, bored and despondent because I have learnt nothing, understood nothing of soap manufacture as the chemists describe it, I stroll around Marseilles: how can I get to know this town? How can I find some way of entering into its life?

Impossible to make anything of it from the outside— poverty looms up so stark, so massive that one cannot see past it, and it seems to me that the various "solutions" people put forward, so far from being dictated by the facts, are simply pinned onto a reality which they know nothing about.

Even the population is in doubt; "a million or two", says an official handbook, content to guess to the nearest million;

650,000, 700,000, 800,000, surmise the statisticians, with scarcely less diffidence.

Conduct statistical analyses? There have been scores of them, and they tell us precisely nothing. In the struggle to get behind this poverty to the people themselves, there is, in fact, only one way which so far the sociologists haven't tried: living in it themselves.

Consequently, I concluded, it was no good wasting time on paper theories: the thing to do was to buy an overall on the old-clothes market, get a job like everyone else, and then, at the end of the day's work, go off and live with the very dregs of the population—the dockers on the ports.

I announce that I want to work on the wharves. I am told, "You're taking on the impossible—dockers are the toughest section of any community, and as for those of Marseilles, why, they're dockers plus . . . you've picked on the most evil and terrible fellows in the world."

And it is quite true that scarcely has one donned a pair of patched dungarees, filthied by coal and corroded by phosphates or pyrites, than one is thrust into a completely different social category, in the very heart of the proletariat. Get into a tram and people will back away from you a little, covered as you are with coal-dust and grime and, for all they know, lice. If you have to go and explain something to one of the authorities—social insurance, compensation, even the Syndicate itself—the official at the counter invariably begins by abusing you because you're a docker, because you're sure to be out to wangle something, because obviously your "papers" won't be in order. Ah, those papers, what a headache they are! Children often spend half their youth standing in queues, trying to get their parents' papers fixed up.

Before long, I lose any self-possession that I might have had, and when I myself am trying to explain something to these officials I feel they have every excuse for abusing me, and that I am in truth a thoroughly low type.

At work, on the other hand, the fraternity of the working classes comes into full play. I succeed in getting a huge foreman to take me on, despite his remark that I look pretty awkward. Actually, he is short of men to unload a number of fifty pound sacks of semolina. As I watch these enormous sacks leaving the side of the ship, I feel a bit uneasy. I tell the man next to me, "You know, I've never done this job before. . . ." I go up to the platform, about the height of my head; someone rolls the sack onto my shoulders—I almost fold up like a concertina—then I set off, first right, then left . . . finally at the second turn the sack slides over my head and onto the ground.

Instantly, these dockers—dogged as they are by insecurity, for competition is fierce—instead of feeling any sort of resentment against the newcomer out to compete with them, think only of the poor bloke who doesn't know how to go about the job. Four men promptly pick up the sack and toss it on the shoulders of a fifth, who carries on in my place.

Thus these workers, who are quite ready to cut their employers' throats, instinctively show a feeling of solidarity, of fraternal charity in the fullest sense of the word for the maladroit newcomer.

They shower me with questions: "Are you sick?" "What went wrong?" and give me useful tips on working methods. But the foreman sacks me; nor am I sorry, for I tell myself that four more hours of work like that would finish me.

My companions of a half-hour suggest I try coal-docking: "It isn't too heavy, quite slight chaps can do it. Dirty, of course. At the end of it, no one would guess you were a human being at all."

Each working day on the wharves opens my eyes a little

more to the results of an inhuman labour-contract policy. At every moment I witness a peculiarly working-class anomaly, the counterpart to an equally extreme expression of capitalism.

Here are men who are signed on for four hours only at a time, who never know in the morning if they will have a job in the afternoon.[1] At the end of thirty years, they are no more at home in the port than on the second or third day of their arrival from Spain or wherever they came from. They are keenly conscious of being regarded as mere tools. The first battle to be won for the working-class is the battle for the right to work. An old Spanish docker will shout in his sleep, "Ah! they're going to fire me because I'm a foreigner! . . ." and when he hits out it is his wife who suffers the blow.

I find the port divided into two sections: on the one hand, the men who enjoy all the profits and none of the risks, and on the other, those whose sole portion is the risks: in other words, the dockers. It rains, the boat isn't unloaded; or again, the boats don't arrive; in either case, they are out of work. At Marseilles the railway-lines are so narrow that it sometimes takes twenty-four hours' manoeuvring to get a truck from one point to another. The day when the S.N.C.F.[2] is late, the docker is idle. Every inopportune event, rain, storm, it doesn't matter what, is always felt by the docker in terms of unemployment and worry.

Thus, in the course of unloading phosphates, pyrites, groundnuts, cork, coal, I perceive gradually, but always from the inside, that unless these problems are successfully tackled at the root, all other reform projects will be useless

---

[1] Since the Liberation—and perhaps partly due to missionary efforts in this direction—the labour contract system has been considerably improved.
[2] Translator's note: the French National Railway System.

—normal human development for these men will be out of question. I see likewise, and again from the inside, the real meaning of the law of profit, the one ruling force in the harbour area and its neighbouring wharves. Everyone is dominated by one fear: a ship must never be kept waiting to be unloaded. Too bad if that involves supernumeraries who will only be employed in rush periods, too bad if the rest of the time they starve: the crime is not that men should starve but that a ship should be held up.

Later I shall be able to return to figures and statistics, for they, too, are necessary; but then I shall know what lies behind each curve of the graph, because I have heard for myself the heavy step of the docker who, for lack of work, returns home barely two hours after he set out. I have taken part a score of times in this wordless little drama: the man throwing down his rucksack, shrugging his shoulders, silent before the wife whose anxious ears so dreaded hearing the familiar step, and who now sits with constricted heart: another day to face with no money. The man feels guilty; and yet—what can he do about it?

Some months later, the following incident confirms, if confirmation were needed, that certain chains of social cause and effect are as determined and inescapable as the laws of physics and chemistry. A woman comes to summon me. She is stout, with swollen legs; she is obviously in great distress: "Come with me, things are bad at home." I follow her. What a scene of desolation! In a family of eight, four including the mother have had typhoid. The eldest of the boys is so weak that he is a mass of sores and bruises from falling down the stairs. There is one bed and a straw mattress between the lot of them, barely two whole chairs, the gas is cut off, the rusty saucepan long unused. The father is a docker. He says he wants work but that he can't succeed

B

in getting signed on. He and I chat for a long time. So it is really true, then, that a man who genuinely wants work can't manage to get it. . . .

Some days later a steady job offers. It pays less than work on the wharves, but it is regular daily employment. Then, solely thanks to this new-found security, gradually the family recovers, for all the world like a thirsty bunch of flowers steeped in water. The children grow stronger, the mother regains her pride in keeping house. Two, three, four beds are bought. At the end of a year each child can sit down on its own chair—and all that, simply because the question of daily bread no longer hinged on the daily "signing on" problem.

I discover at the same time the extent to which the slum problem is bound up with the labour-contract system; the congestion of certain families in miserable courtyards some hundreds of yards from the harbour is the inevitable consequence of conditions of employment.

That abolishing slums means first changing the method of hiring labour is something that I shall never tire of urging. And this, the one essential preliminary, is precisely what the employers prefer not to understand. If they were told, "One, two, ten thousand pounds are needed for a social centre", they would produce the money in five minutes, but as soon as someone says to them, "You must revise the contract system", he runs up against a brick wall.

Meanwhile, I am acutely aware that a whole side of the docker's life, and what should be the best part of it, is escaping me. Working with him isn't enough—at the end of the day's work, instead of returning to the monastery, I should be going back with him and living as a worker among the workers; for man's needs are not solely material, he thirsts, too, for love and affection, and where does he normally find these?

At mealtimes in the canteen, where we number some four or five hundred, I am struck by the faces around me—they have no expression. I look for something, no matter what, anything from hate to desire, just some reflection of humanity —but every face is blank as if each wore a mask; I get the impression that something has been deliberately shut away and locked.

However, after dinner some of us go into a little *bistro*. The proprietress comes out, a real Marseillaise, friendly, welcoming, light-hearted. We are tired, we've dropped in for a glass of wine before going back to work. Suddenly, at the appearance of the little girl who brings in the cups of watery coffee, makes some polite little remark, touches one's hand or one's shoulder—well, all at once the mask drops and one sees these men's eyes become clear and child-like, shining for a few seconds with all the unexpressed love in their hearts. That, when one has seen it for oneself, is unforgettable.

Again, that same evening I accompany a friend to his home. He lives in a hovel, a hole of a place for which he pays a hundred and ninety francs a month,[1] the trodden earth for floor, no window, no coal cellar, no closet, no anything: sure, I saw the paliasse where he begot his youngsters, but was this a place where love, where family affection could flourish? They live in fourteen square yards. There are five persons, and a single room has to serve as bedroom, kitchen, dining-room, coal-cellar, lavatory and anything over and above.

It is a hell-hole. How could family love thrive there?

One thing stands firm in this rout of the human affections: paternal tenderness. My comrade with his great calloused hands picks up the little three-month-old, teases and plays

[1] In 1939–43.

with it with all the delicacy of the gentlest of mothers. Yes, that survives—that survives just as long as the youngster is small. As soon as it grows a bit, delight turns into irritation. The kid starts getting under your feet. While it is little, you can still manage to tuck it in a corner of the bed or in a cupboard drawer, but soon it becomes just one more person taking up space in a home which is already over-crowded.

Dungarees, manual labour—prerequisites for the rediscovery and rescue of man!

CHAPTER II

Living Together

So I obtain permission from my superiors to go and live twenty-four hours a day with the most derelict classes in Marseilles, and, having resumed my Dominican habit, set out to install myself in the district of V.2, in the very midst of the port-workers, rag-and-bone dealers and gypsies.

But it is harder to gain admittance to the intimate life of these people than it is to get work. For many weeks I look for a place. I don't ask much, but even to find a few square yards under a roof isn't easy. One day a good woman explains: "I don't fancy the idea of someone setting fire to the place because there's a priest inside."

At last I find a lodging and I arrive with a bucket of lime to whitewash the room. Opinion on seeing me settle in is rather divided. A tiny minority of old women who still keep a rosary in the bottom of their purses are pleased: "A priest here, eh? Well, after all, it isn't right that only the rich should have them!"

The great majority are dumbfounded, as if a man from the moon had settled in their midst. "A priest here—for Pete's sake!" And finally another minority, saying: "Huh! Someone will land him a good kick in the pants—that'll teach him to come here!"

As a matter of fact, the kick never came, and a fortnight after my arrival I'm beginning to form friendly enough relations with all the men in the alley. There is no longer any constraint between us, and very soon, even, real ties of affection are set up with the more immediate neighbours.

I verify the fact that there is an order in hatred just as there is an order in charity. Hatred, when it is not nourished by personal motives, fades in the presence of its object, and in the familiarly shared context of daily life. When a neighbour wants to meet me for the first time, he doesn't come when I am sitting at home. Although he only has to push the door, he chooses instead the moment when I am walking back from the well, because then he finds me even more accessible. When a housewife says to me, "Ha! I saw you at the baker's this morning," well, I am truly part and parcel of the district. I am no longer a mysterious priest, I have become someone who is genuinely one of themselves, someone whose comings and goings they can mark. Similarly, when they do come to my door, it is always when I am in the middle of a meal and they can see what I am eating.

But at the same time, I am becoming aware of the limits of what individual human effort can achieve. The more one withdraws from the point where one actually lives, the more impersonal one's action becomes. It will be important later to define these limits.

At the end of six weeks I fall ill and have to leave the district. A neighbour's comment: "This priest is like the rest—living with us is too tough for him." But when I return after eight weeks' absence and definitely settle in again, they realise that I am there for good. Even men I didn't know greeted me cordially, complete strangers hailed me—in short, I am accepted.

In August and September 1943, the Germans order the evacuation of the district. This is catastrophe indeed, and just as if someone had kicked over a giant ant-hill. Some leave for Ardèche, others look for some sort of accommodation in the town. I in my turn set out to establish myself in another district.

This time, finding a room is much easier than before. In the tram I run into a woman who keeps a sweet-shop, whom I don't actually know but who had often noticed me (thanks to my habit), and whose face is vaguely familiar.

"Well, Father, and what are you doing here?"

"I'm looking for lodgings."

"Come home with me, there's an empty room in one of the courtyards—maybe the landlord will let it to you. Let's go straightaway—it's nine o'clock so he's still in bed. He sleeps late."

I hear the conversation:

Madame Sidonie: "He's a priest, mind you, Said", (the landlord is an Arab), "a white priest, but a priest just the same."

The religious aspect doesn't bother Said much:

"You think he'll pay the rent?"

"Oh yes, he'll pay it all right."

"You're quite sure?"

"I can guarantee it."

"Oh, well, then, show him up."

I am admitted to a bedside audience with my future landlord.

"You have to pay in advance, you know. . . ."

"Yes, I shall pay you in advance."

"Well, that's O.K., then."

The smell pervading the room is characteristically stale and fetid. Veterans soon learn to detect by sense of smell the rooms whose walls house bed-bugs and cockroaches, and to distinguish them "at a sniff" from those which merely ooze dirt.

The nose gets used to it, but the eye is ill at ease all the time: it has forgotten what it is like to see an horizon. You need to be myopic, for invariably at seven or eight feet, ten at the most, a wall cuts short your field of vision. When, after many months passed thus, you happen to find yourself enjoying a distant view, you suddenly realise what was missing: the satisfaction of the eye's need to focus farther off. And you find out, too, that the only way of regularly humouring these tricks of the retina is by going to the cinema to see some Hawaiian or Wild West film.

Smell, sight, touch—constantly irritated by parasites; hearing—continually assaulted by sudden outbreaks of quarrelling and children crying: the senses are put on severe trial. But can a house be certified as insanitary on these grounds? Alas, no! "Insanitary—that which causes illness"; everyone is well aware that people die in these places four, five, ten times more quickly than elsewhere, but what statistics can convey the sound of those early morning catarrhal or tubercular coughs?

Engels, in *The Position of the Working Classes in England in the Nineteenth Century* (the first of the great flood of Communist works which were to come), gives a detailed description of the Manchester slum yards. Here, the picture has scarcely changed.

The yard in which we live, about sixty of us, is forty-eight by twelve yards, ground and huts included. Each room is eleven feet high and under ten feet square. The rents are exorbitant: a hundred and fifty to a hundred and eighty francs a month for an empty ten by ten room, without water, without gas, without toilet; often without electricity. Three hundred and fifty to four hundred francs a month if this room is blessed with furniture, i.e. some iron bedsteads without mattresses, whose sole adornment is clusters of bed-bugs.[1] Add on eighty or a hundred francs per month for tram-fares,

---

[1] Note: these rents applied in 1943–4. In 1946 they were respectively from three hundred francs unfurnished, and from eight hundred francs furnished.

and it will be seen that it is the worst lodged who pay proportionately the highest.

The fact is that one is confronted here by an institution exactly like that of ancient slavery. In our courtyard, three-fifths of the earnings of the inhabitants go into the landlord's pocket. He, as it happens, keeps a bar-restaurant; if you want to rent a room you are obliged to have your meals there, or, at the very least, go there for your drinks. Conversely, non-lodgers who want to eat in the restaurant are given the choice of renting a room or eating somewhere else.

If one adds to this the loans which the landlord grants in moments of financial embarrassment, and which he gets back at heavy interest, and finally if one considers that he supplies his tenants through the black market with everything they are able to buy, one realises that here in actual fact is an enterprise whereby fifty or so people work for the ultimate enrichment of one man. Of course, each retains in theory his liberty, i.e. he can go and sign on where he pleases, but wasn't this so with the ancient slave, the craftsman who was free in his movements or in the conduct of his little business, but who none the less handed over all the fruits of his labour to his master? As for the women slaves, one can make a fair guess what use was made of them.

In the yard, we all live, as it were, in bulk, with no windows, or practically none, a door certainly, but one which shuts out neither noise nor bad weather. A little calm sets in between 12.30 and 4 a.m., provided that some drunk doesn't come in singing, according to his age, "*Viens Poupoule*" (if that was popular in his youth) or some Tino Rossi verses.

On top of these insanitary, "bulk" living conditions comes the problem of over-crowding. It has been talked about often

enough, but this also must be seen at close quarters. Daniel is
three, Zezette two and a half, two neighbours who enjoy
playing together; but when they play Fathers and Mothers,
the game is not confined to make-believe tea-parties and
"visiting", but includes that which constitutes the true paternal and maternal functions, i.e. engendering other little
Daniels and other little Zezettes. They do it in all innocence
of course, ingenuously reproducing scenes which the over-
crowding renders common and inevitable.

The demolition of slums is a fine subject for decrees or
propaganda, but it doesn't come about as easily as people
think, and when demolition is not preceded by any construction the remedy is worse than the evil. A few years ago
a government agent came to Marseilles to proceed with the
pulling down of condemned houses; there was no question,
of course, of laying the foundation stone of any new building,
but simply of demolishing some little blocks of houses which
threatened to collapse.

Everything was nicely organised: at the first place the
official merely had to press a lever, and amidst a great
crashing and clouds of dust and debris, a surface crack in
the main hall gave way.

The battle had started. In the next yard, they had
thought to vary the visitor's entertainment: instead of pressing a lever he had to operate a winch, but in this case the
wall showed resistance (this was during the occupation); it
refused to budge, and the winch, carried away by its own
momentum, shot towards the wall: a fitting symbol of the
difficulties involved in the demolition of condemned blocks.

But it is imperative that we draw a lesson from these
slums before we pull them down, at any rate from those
which have developed of their own accord without help
from the architects. If hygiene is non-existent in them, if

the sewer drain runs down the middle of the street, nevertheless the human, social character of these places is generally speaking much more marked than in the majority of cheap lodging houses.

The *bistro* is a veritable social centre, replacing the parish in the spiritual sphere and the social assistant in the temporal. When the postman comes to 78 Boulevard F2, he is quite baffled to know how to deliver his mail. All the inhabitants are Spaniards, Algerians or Armenians, and all seem to bear the same names. How is he to distinguish Fernandez from Fernandez, Martinez from Martinez, Kajadjian from Kajadjian? The two hundred families in the enclosure all live at No 78, which represents the main entrance to the patch of wasteland where they have built their shanties; so if the postman makes the mistake of bawling out a name into the yard, ten claimants step forward, all answering to it. In despair, the postman then goes to the pub-keeper, who knows his little world very well and who will be able—by heaven knows what powers of divination—to pass the letter on to the right person; moreover, if the latter cannot write, the pub-keeper will reply for him.

After that, it is easier to understand this multiplicity of bars and wine-dealers, so well described by Léon Frapié in *La Maternelle*: "Out of twenty shops one may count fourteen wine-shops and four second-hand dealers. There are restaurant-wine-shops, grocer-wine-shops, fruiterer-wine-shops, dairy-wine-shops, tobacco-wine-shops, concert-wine-shops and popular dance-halls, coal-merchant-wine-shops, the 'bar', the distillery—each one providing furnished lodgings." Add now to this list the dealers in black-market wines. . . .

Thus the little shanty town organises itself into a proper community, the houses following the one-story pattern universally favoured by the peoples of the Mediterranean.

Balthazar, who is a docker, lived with his wife for twenty years in one of these houses. At eight o'clock in the evening, after supper, he used to take his chair outside, straddle it over the drain and rock himself to and fro, enjoying the cool of the evening. A few feet away, his wife did the washing-up while the children played in the alley; the other neighbours would come out likewise, and until ten or ten-thirty the men yarned about their work, their troubles and joys. At ten or thereabouts they would go in to bed because they had risen early, and then it was the women's turn to come out and gossip until nearly midnight.

But the whole block having been reported unfit for habitation, all the residents were evacuated. For some days everyone bustles around trying to find lodgings, which will, in the end, be more unhealthy and congested than the ones they have left.

Balthazar, however, had the unheard-of good luck—so he thought, anyway—of finding a diminutive flat on the fourth story of a modern house, complete with tiny kitchen, tiny bedroom, a tiny recess for the children—but then what was one to do in the evenings in this cramped little fly-trap of a place, suspended between heaven and earth? Balthazar takes his cap and goes down to the doorstep for his evening breath of air. From now on, four stories separate him from his wife. She is left on her own to attend to the household chores, and the children—having no more reason for staying with their father than with their mother—go off on their own. In three weeks, the family group, hitherto so closely bound together, has fallen apart, and Balthazar resorts to the *bistro*—but one which is quite unlike the sociable *bistro* of the old days where one wasn't even obliged to drink.

CHAPTER III

Making Contact

I INSTALL myself gradually. My nearest neighbour is a working-class prostitute, a poor woman who would like nothing better than to settle down in life, but whose bad housekeeping rapidly discourages one "husband" after another.

Opposite is the family with whom I shall live in the closest possible intimacy for two years: one room, as usual, doing duty for a whole house, lavatory included. The family consists of a grandfather, a grandmother, and a little girl of twelve.

Everything that it has been possible to accumulate in the course of seventy years in the way of old tools, rickety furniture, coats of dirt, old photo-frames, fly specks, is all heaped up there. If you want something, you have to get it out of one of the boxes piled under the bed, but to move the bed you must first get the table out of the way. Saucepans and food go on the floor because there's nowhere else to put them.

Good morning, good evening—our relations scarcely go beyond that. One day about twelve, Madame Antoine, having just made a fine fish noodle soup, sends me in a plate by her little girl. Some weeks later, I become her boarder; a little later still, we are all four living together, having our two rooms in common.

It is only then that, little by little, as when a mist begins to thin, the true countenance and the deep personal life of the Antoine family is revealed to me.

Madame Antoine is French; furthermore, she is Provençal, and that gives her, in the midst of all the foreigners, a real superiority. As a hostess, she clearly owes nothing to the etiquette books, but her courtesy is all the more genuine for that reason. When we receive visitors, one feels that she regards the maintenance of conversation as her personal responsibility.

She expresses herself in homely axioms: "Bread on the table knows no owner", says she to a supper guest who, in times of severe rationing, hesitates to take another piece. If the talk turns on the grave problems of world politics: "Men are all equal. . . . When one of them is wounded, whether he is French, German, Russian or American, whether he's black or white, isn't his blood always red?"

She came to Marseilles at the age of seventeen, and has never moved out of it; her life has passed in the same neighbourhood and in the same poky little dwellings which aged more quickly than she did herself, dying one by one of decrepitude. From all the people she has mixed with, from all the events she has lived through, she has drawn a philosophy which can be summed up in two or three articles: "Have nothing to do with the police", "No good ever comes of a woman who drinks"—these are the negative postulates. As for the positive side, she expresses that to me one day when a louder brawl than usual has just broken out in the yard: "Look, Father, if we all truly loved our neighbours, well, the war, the Boches, even the rationing would be nothing. But loving each other . . . that's not easy." And she adds, as she always does in moments of great solemnity, "Ah, yes, by the head of my poor Ernest, that's by no means easy." (Ernest was her deceased first husband.)

Having been in domestic service in her youth, she explains

what an advantage this is for young girls: "It teaches them a great deal they would never learn at home, and seeing how their employers behave helps them to know how to treat their husbands later on." She says that with a mischievous smile and a glance at her husband, and I translate: "It helps them to know how to order their husbands about as they please. . . ." In any case, Monsieur Antoine is less subtle than his wife. Provided he finds his tobacco and a bottle of wine waiting for him when he comes back from work, he is content.

But this is still only a surface view of the Antoine family. At the end of six months I am thoroughly familiar with the customs of this old couple, their little fads, their joys and their grouses. And by that time, they had come to remind me very much of another family which I also know from the inside. I see beyond the indescribable dirt and disorder—so inevitable!—and cease to notice them: Madame Antoine and her husband are amazingly like my own father and mother, whom I see again in imagination in their comfortable, beautifully kept flat.

Besides, Madame Antoine has adopted me as a son; she worries when she sees me looking tired, and prepares special snail broths to revive me.

When neighbours or others come to see me, they find me *en famille*, and I receive them indifferently in my room or that of the Antoines.

I am truly part of the district, although I often leave it at six or seven in the morning and only return late in the evening, since I am still busying myself in the town on economic and social questions. But the fact of sleeping there, of being in the true and juridical sense of the word domiciled in the district, makes my position enormously different from what it would be if I spent the whole day working for the district,

but disappeared every evening to go and sleep at the
monastery.

The first and most important effect of this nightly habitat
is that it precludes any kind of hypocrisy. We really do share
the same life because we suffer the same difficulties, the same
troubles, and drink the same wine, often from the same glass.
And this is where the real social and religious problems are
to be met—not in complicated theoretical abstractions, but
in simple questions devolving on lice and such things.

Some girls have not made their First Communion; they
cannot read; they will be outcasts all their lives. Why?
Because they had lice on their scalps when they were kids!
Mother refuses to shave the child's head (having lice isn't
so very shameful, but to have one's hair shaved off is real
disgrace) and consequently the little one doesn't go to school,
since the teacher objects to lice; nor will it go to catechism
class for fear of being put to shame by the priest.

Here are children whose whole lives will be spoilt. What
is to be done? It is quite simple—remove the lice and gently
set the child back on the right track. That is where social
service and the religious life dedicated to social service should
begin. What progress already when the child cries—"Look
I haven't got any more lice on my head, no more nits . . . !"

François is another neighbour; he is tall, too tall, his arms
are too long, his legs never seem to come to an end. He is a
rag-and-bone dealer and shares a room with Marguerite,
the rag-and-bone woman; she is much older than he is, but
every night he conscientiously unrolls a palliasse for her on
the ground.

A very great, very rich friendship exists between François
and myself. After many months, he tells me that he has
possessed neither ration cards nor an identity card for a very

long time. "It isn't as awkward as you'd think, except that sugar and coffee are a bit hard to get." And he asks me if I could possibly get hold of these papers for him.

Why, yes, he has been several times to the commissioner of police, but he has always been chased away and he daren't worry them again.

The next day, I in my turn go to the commissariat. I am shown the list of formalities to be met, enough to keep one busy for three months. Then I go to the *Service Central de la Statistique Municipale et du Ravitaillement*. I go from one counter to another and end up at No. 8, where I join the queue.

The assistant is in an extremely bad temper and one housewife after another goes away crestfallen because she lacks a birth-certificate or some stamp or other on one of her forms. I say to myself, "I'm done for, not a hope, I'll never manage to get anything whatsoever!"

But in Marseilles perseverance is not the most notable characteristic, and even bad temper cannot last long. I have the good luck to strike a change of mood, and explain my business to one Mademoiselle Viviane whose name is inscribed on her little heart-shaped brooch. She questions me:

"But how does he live then?"

"He not only lives but he manages to feed a dog and a canary as well."

This wins Mademoiselle Viviane and she hands me a collection of forms. Two hours later I have the identity card and everything.

That evening I have a hasty supper and, overjoyed, go off to see François. We hug each other. "Ah! Father, we can't let this pass without a drink." Marguerite rinses out the glasses but doesn't dry them pointing out that the bountiful stock of rags on the premises are a bit unsuitable for house-hold use.

We clink glasses to the prospect of the good things that the ration cards will provide. But François has a strong social sense. So long as we haven't eaten salt together there is no true friendship; wine itself doesn't suffice. François invites me to supper.

"Father, we must eat together."

"I'd love to, but tomorrow evening; I've already had supper."

"No, tonight, tomorrow won't be the same thing; what we're celebrating will be already past—it's this evening we must eat together."

I refuse; he insists. Plainly he is looking for the clinching argument:

"Look, Father, you needn't worry, there's nothing in the soup today except what I found in the garbage-tins . . . so make yourself at home."

The argument makes retort impossible: there remains nothing for it but to sit down to table. The first spoonful goes down with difficulty, after that it is plain sailing; the soup isn't as bad as all that, with a good dose of red pepper. Scraps of slightly rancid bacon swim on the surface. François is heart-broken because he wasn't able to find any of the little dead rabbits that he often puts into the stock-pot.

Such is our first close contact with each other.

One evening in spring, François comes along: "Listen, Father, I'd like to make my First Communion." He is thirty-two. Every night for four months François comes when things have quietened down and the majority of my visitors have gone home to bed.

Together we read all the Gospels without skipping a word,

including St. John. He grasps it magnificently. He and his companion make real efforts. The great obstacle—but is it really, if one goes to the root of things?—is the bottle.

Marguerite likewise comes one day—one Monday: "Father, I'd like to receive Communion on Sunday, and so I want to go to confession, but not till Saturday. I think it's better to leave it until the day before."

We chat for a bit.

"All the same, you know, it's a pity you drink too much!"

"Listen, Father, I promise I won't get drunk all this week."

That is plain heroism, and as a matter of fact she keeps her word. I meet her each evening: "You see, you see, I'm keeping my promise." It is true that sometimes she says it with an agitation which leaves me a little sceptical.

On Sunday Marguerite goes to Communion. She had communicated occasionally before: in hospital, in prison, but never really of her own free will, always under the influence of some nun who had more or less pushed her; her joy knew no bounds on this Sunday morning, after this wholly voluntary action of hers, and she kept repeating as her *leit motiv*: "You know, Father, this time I went to Communion because I really wanted to, and it's the first time I ever have."

Meanwhile, François is getting ready. We always read the Gospels, then we pray in dialogue, each offering up all his intentions; finally, we embrace and part.

The 15th of August draws near; this is the day when François is to make his First Communion. His neighbours and close friends in the yard know all about it. Each day François grows in Christian stature: he is solicitous for the apostolate and the community, of which he desires to be the foremost member.

Suddenly, catastrophe. We are in the days preceding the Allied landing in Provence. Food supplies in Marseilles grow worse and worse; lacking bread, lacking vegetables, the authorities have found no better solution than to replace the missing rations with extra quotas of wine.

It is easy to imagine the effect produced on a hungry populace. How could François have stood out against it? And when he has drunk the quart ration, he simply has to add another quart from the black market.

On the 9th of August, he creates an appalling scandal in the yard: he shouts, howls, fights, his goods are removed at midnight—the picture is complete.

The following evening, we meet again for prayer.

"Father, I guess you heard. . . ."

I had. We ask ourselves what should be done.

"Listen, François, it is impossible to found a Christian community like that; it can't be done. To be sure, God forgives you straight away if you ask Him, but what are the people in the yard going to say—the people who look to you as a Christian?"

"That's true; they'll say, 'So that's a Christian for you!'"

"You can't possibly make your Communion in five days' time."

François is repentant from the bottom of his heart, weeps, pressing his head against the crucifix.

"Ah well, I suppose it would be better to put it off a few weeks. . . ."

We decide that his Communion will take place on the 8th of September, the Nativity of the Blessed Virgin.

The Allied troops approach. General pillage throughout the whole district of the big shops and warehouses. Everyone does it, and it is just as well, for otherwise we should have starved to death in the days that followed.

The Germans fire on the crowd. François is too big, he towers over the others by a head. Wounded and taken to hospital, he dies there a few days before his First Communion.

But surely it is in Heaven itself that he will receive Christ in Communion, this poor, wretched, outcast child, assuming the splendid title of the son of God, receiving his heritage. . . .

Clairette is eighteen, a big, fair girl with straight and wiry hair like drum-sticks, not always very tidy; she often comes to see me with her mother and brother, for her bad character involves her in a fair number of brawls in the district. Besides, there are other troubles—the eldest brother is fighting with the Free French, a sister died last year. . . .

One fine day she informs me that she is going to marry an Arab. That alarms me, I have already seen two French girls die under Arab blows. But the fiancé is an exception, a very likeable lad albeit a good deal darker than most of his compatriots.

The marriage of Ali and Clairette is arranged amidst canonical and administrative difficulties. It is agreed that the children will be Christians, and parleys take place with the diocesan secretary on the matter of dispensations. Everything is ready, but on the point of receiving her *livret de famille*, she and the canon fall into violent argument.

"That's just too bad; Father will marry us without you and your papers," declares Clairette.

The canon on his side reacts vigorously, and next day I have to reconcile all parties and search through the wastepaper basket for the torn-up marriage forms.

On the Saturday of the wedding, Ali has to sign his commitments in the matter of the religious education of the children. At the moment of signing, he raises a distinction: "The girls can be Catholics, sure, that's not important, the

girls can go to the devil if they please! But the boys—
Mahommedans.''

This is not bad faith on his part, he hadn't properly understood up till then what was required of him. I tell him that
the Church is adamant on this point. Ali is not the man to
give his word lightly:

"Listen, I must have eight days to think about it. If
you like, we'll get married tonight at the town hall and then
in eight days' time we'll see about the Church.''

But Clairette, seized by unexpected zeal, proceeds to com-
plicate the situation for him: "The town hall and the church
tonight, or nothing at all.''

Ali asks to be allowed to reflect until 1.30 p.m. (the civil
marriage is fixed for 3 p.m.). We separate, and Clairette
goes off to give herself a superb "perm''. She reappears at
1.30 p.m. as curly and frizzy as her future spouse.

Ali agrees, he signs the form. Everyone is delighted. The
festal joints are ready to be quartered, and we set off for the
town hall in an open cart.

In these marriages where I am witness at the town hall,
and where the religious ceremony is followed by a wedding
feast, these three aspects form a true whole. In the same way,
no doubt, as in the marriage at Cana, the religious ceremony
and the civil ceremony each assumes its proper importance.
How different from those marriages where an unknown
priest awaits the young couple, who make a quick trip to the
church and then in a quarter of an hour are on their way
again.

But to return to Ali's marriage, I am a bit uneasy about
the wedding feast which is to follow. He keeps a bar and
knows how to do things on the grand scale. Also, a few days
previously Clairette herself said to me, "We shan't have just
a tame party at my fiancé's place; we're going to hire a

room in town." The next day, thinking better of it, she tells me that the party will definitely be held at Ali's home: "It costs too much renting the room in town, and, anyhow, it would be awkward bringing back the drunks—better to have 'em pass out somewhere near home!"

As we leave the church, Clairette's words drum inside my head. Cocktails, liqueurs, then the feast starting at 7 p.m. and continuing until 2 in the morning. . . . As a matter of fact, no one gets drunk; thanks very largely to two women friends from the apostolate who had been invited, we manage to create an atmosphere of family joy and good-fellowship— they sing and play like youngsters, with all the healthy, exuberant gaiety of the childhood which many of them have never had.

However, in the middle of the fun the door opens, and an Arab—the jilted fiancé of one of the girls at the party—comes in: an icy chill descends on everyone, for it seems obvious that he has come to make trouble. He sits on the table, says nothing, and we try to carry on without paying too much attention to him: all at once he rises abruptly, slams the door and departs. A general sigh of relief; this was the only false note in the evening.

The next day, someone runs into him: "Well, what happened to you last night?"

"Oh, I don't know . . . you all seemed so pleased, so happy, I hadn't the heart. I put the gun in the other pocket and left. . . ."

One evening, after six alerts, Madame Emile had just finished arranging a basket of baked apples which she was preparing to sell. A seventh alert sounds—she is in despair, it is impossible to do her round, how will she earn the day's keep? So I suggest that she carry them to the shelter where the whole neighbourhood has taken refuge. "You'll see—everyone who is bored with waiting will buy them!"

We make for the shelter. The people have certainly had enough:

"Father, if there were a good God, we wouldn't see all this going on, there wouldn't be any war and bombers and such things . . ." and just then, it is terribly hard to answer them.

Luckily, Madame Emile starts selling her apples; they disappear at record speed; she is jubilant and shouts to me from the other side of the shelter:

"Ah, Father, it's plain enough there's a good God for honest folk! Three francs an apple, three francs. . . . Ah yes, Father, it's clear there's a good God for the honest."

Isn't this a symbol of that minimum of joy and well-being needed to keep people's hearts open to the things of heaven?

Brotherly contact, the joy of food shared in common, re-discovery of the importance these have in the Gospel, and, at the same time, continual efforts to realise those social reforms whose necessity becomes more manifest at every step—it is in this way that the missionary apostolate realises the scriptural comparison: "the just shall flourish like the palm"—the palm whose head is in the open sky, in the sunshine and bright air (and this is symbolic of the reform of the social structure), but which at the same time is rooted in the kindly moisture of the earth, its tendrils gathering in every least drop of water (and these are all the little events of daily life shared down to the last detail).

Nowhere has this sharing been deeper or more beneficial than at the "Residence", which I must now describe.

CHAPTER IV

Light Shines In The Darkness

THE NECESSITY for organising what later came to be known as the Residence, first became obvious at the Daurane in 1942. In this urban residential centre live a little under two hundred families, mainly Armenian.

Several girls worked among them for three years. They had succeeded in penetrating into the people's lives only very slowly. For nearly a year they had had to be content with seeing shutters on the doors or windows lift slightly at their passing, as the inmates covertly eyed them. And then one day, like a long-smouldering fire which suddenly catches because the wood is at last dry, they were accepted and admitted into the people's homes. This victory was succeeded by a period in which countless claims were made on them, because they were trusted—but trusted only because for many months, every Thursday and Sunday, they had been regularly seen about the neighbourhood.

As for the things required of them, these were of every description: clothes or shoes, baby-minding, holiday camps, difficulties to be smoothed over with the police or the aliens' branch—it was all one. Thanks to the influence of personal contact, the girls of the locality became neater, the boys less wild. In spite of the characteristically noisy ways of Armenians a certain peace reigned, and one sometimes had the impression that the whole lot of them might well, in time, become quite civilised.

A building enabled parents and children to come together from time to time, e.g. for Mass or festive occasions. In short, the Daurane was a very different place from what it had been two years previously.

This, however, was the most that could be achieved by this method, with its bi-weekly contact. The effective aid which would have seen the permanent relief of certain families, a healthy re-direction in the lives of the young by way of fitting the boys for a trade, the girls for domestic work, continual care for the aged and the helpless sick—all that was impossible. The Daurane was ready to move on to a third stage in its advance, but before it could do so, the creation of some kind of permanent establishment was essential.

Then someone had the idea of setting up a small centre for young workers, but only for those of the immediate neighbourhood: a centre with nothing very academic about it, since the instructors—who would have little enough to do, given the small number of boys and girls between fourteen and eighteen—would attend equally to the biggest and smallest of their pupils, at different times and according to individual needs.

Thus, and without even the knowledge that the thing had already existed elsewhere for many years, actual experience of local, concrete problems and difficulties resulted in the conception of a district residence.

In practice, the idea failed for lack of people prepared to engage in such work full-time, the courageous women who had done the pioneer work in the Daurane being either unwilling or unable to devote all their time to it, or to reside there.

But two points were well established:

1. The need for permanent and stable contacts leading to personal friendships.

2. The creation of a home where this friendship could be transformed into effective help, adapted to the needs of each.

I shall always think of the meeting of Marie S——, Marguerite X—— and myself as a very clear and very precious sign of the Will of God.

One morning in November 1942, introduced by a girl who had seen her at a lecture, arrives Marie S——, militant Jociste, milliner by trade. It is eight o'clock, she is on her way to work.

She invites me to make contact with the district where she lives. Subsequently, thanks to Marie's welcome, and to her family—mother, brothers and sister—who did their best to adopt me, I am accepted by the neighbours, and some months later I settle in the district myself.

What did Marie want? It wasn't easy to determine. She told me of her efforts to help her fellows in this locality of destitutes, foreigners and slums, whose notoriety had already spread to Marseilles through the Press. Here Marie was thoroughly at home: now unofficial secretary, now sick-nurse, always joy and gaiety personified. She wanted to help all these people to climb out of their rut, and above all to avoid what she herself had suffered from so much: loneliness, the lack of an outstretched hand—offering, not money (which pride would have resented), but assistance in getting over some difficult patch, in gaining access to books and education.

Consequently, although she belonged in everyone's eyes to the "priests' party", Marie was unanimously approved in this ardently Communist neighbourhood.

As for Marguerite X——, I had already met her once: she had wanted to live in the midst of the poor, the workers, becoming a worker herself in an ordinary wage-earning job, working half the day in order to devote the rest of her time to her neighbours.

Thus Marguerite and Marie confirmed my belief in the necessity and incomparable benefits of ordinary, day-to-day contacts, of an immersion in the life of the proletariat. Actually, it was less with the proletariat than with the sub-proletariat that they were both concerned: aliens, Spaniards or Italians on the one hand, gipsies on the other, easy to approach as soon as one lives with them, but almost impossible to do anything for unless one is constantly on the spot, helping them not to slip back.

Mady A——, head of a girls' school, stood for another tradition and another vision. She had little time for individual action, her sympathies were all for team-work and for the creation, in the poor quarter, of a well-equipped centre where cultural leisure pursuits held pride of place.

It is Marie and Mady who, somewhere about June 1943, sketch between them the first rough plan of the Residence. Mady's notions and personality greatly alarm Marie. "She's a highbrow," says she; "she doesn't understand the working-class—she's always putting her foot in it, thinks she can change people to suit her own ideas; she goes too fast." And Mady, on her side: "She has always worked as an isolated individual; she has no idea of team-work nor concerted social action."

Actually, each appreciated the qualities of her future companion, but the combination didn't work. It was decided that, lacking a building in the locality—something all but impossible to procure—we should start with a holiday camp, successor to that already organised for the local children by a couple of girls the year before.

It was at that point that the Germans ordered the evacuation of the whole district, thus upsetting our plans and giving the holiday camp project a much greater importance, since whole families had to leave their homes. One could see then the extent of Marie's profound influence on the people, not only because of her personal qualities but also because everybody knew her. Her house became the rallying centre. When the two refugee columns moved to Ardèche, her mere presence gave people a feeling of security—indeed no one had any sense of setting out at random, simply because they felt they were not alone, that at every moment there was someone to whom they could say: "Mademoiselle Marie, do you think I should bring the mattress?" "Mademoiselle Marie, what's to be done with this?" etc.

At the same time, in the face of so many worries, difficulties, griefs, one felt that this all-important spiritual help should be supplemented by a material organisation, if one didn't wish to be a mere ray of sunlight giving momentary comfort to people tossed about and drowning in the storm.

As for the school holiday camp, it underwent its second test. Hastily improvised into classes without any real understanding of the children or of the district from which they had come, it seems to have been—in spite of Mady's self-sacrificing efforts—quite disastrous. Mutiny, scenes, screaming, complaints to parents: it was evident that, organised into groups, these little Marseillaises were impossible to control, illustrating one more truth, viz., that the child should be left in his familiar surroundings, that artificial re-groupings must at all costs be avoided. Take, for instance, Mimi, whom I knew for a sweet, timid, affectionate child, and who went for a walk in the country with no clothes on just to enrage the teachers. However, the children always distinguished between Mady and her colleagues, and exempted her from their sworn hatred for all teachers.

It had been decided with Marie that she should go to Lourdes for the Rosary pilgrimage in autumn 1943. She went, and it is there that the meeting between Marguerite and Marie took place—the real starting-point of the Residence. After a few minutes passed together by the shrine, they seemed to have known one another all their lives. Their response to the common people was identical, their ideas on the kind of life they wanted to live, their sympathies and ways of thought were in complete harmony; yes, we shall always cherish the memory of that cool October afternoon when, beneath the gaze of Our Lady, this dedication to a common task was declared.

It was settled that we should go to Paris in order to work out in detail our ideas on future residences. I had, in fact, contacted various people in the first half of 1943, continually obsessed by the residence theory which seemed the sole effective solution of all the experiments so far tried in this domain.

The visit that we made to Paris, Marguerite, Marie, another companion and myself, showed that we were still a long way from our goal.

Our experience at the residence at X—— was a complete failure, in the opinion of Marguerite and Marie. Immense courtyards, over-spacious premises, chilly living quarters, nothing—not even the leisure-time amenities—could impress them.

We felt more at ease at Y——, where the building was more snug and homely. But what a snubbing we got as soon as the woman who received us realised that we were not official, qualified social workers, but just well-meaning amateurs. Having had to fight to defend the work of her foundress friend, Mademoiselle Z——, having been forced—certainly only after a grave crisis and many hesitations—to agree to the appointment of herself and her colleagues as official assistants to the area, her attitude was logical. But from all the things she said to us, Marguerite, Marie and Anne-Marie retained one dominant impression: that whereas in the old days Mademoiselle Z—— and her assistants were just "good neighbours", united to the local inhabitants by ties of friendship, their successors had replaced these friendly ties with semi-official relations which made all real contact impossible.

The encounter with Mademoiselle N—— was much easier. Her fine hospital was a most attractive place, but here again how far one was from the little house where Mademoiselle M——, the foundress, had started making contact with her neighbourhood.

I ask: "But how many people are there in your district?" And the reply, given as only a Parisian knows how, quite simply, without turning a hair: "Seventy thousand." As if a district of seventy thousand inhabitants wasn't one of the thirty-five cities of France!

With the Abbé Godin, the debate (for he loved an argument, the dear, great Abbé) centred upon this point: are the material services that the residences can provide a help or a hindrance to the missionary apostolate?

For the Abbé, the answer was in no doubt: they were unquestionably an embarrassment. And he cited in favour of his thesis the Jocist organisations in the deported workers' camps in Germany, where they had been forced, he said, to divide their services into two kinds: for the man who filled this or that material rôle (postal deliveries, say, or food distribution) was less well placed to preach the Gospel than his comrade who had nothing weighing on him save this one duty.

Again, he gave the example of an organisation he had seen something of in Paris: a service for young married couples, where the person in charge of helping the young home-makers to equip their households with sideboards, table-cloths, saucepans, etc., would hardly find time to urge them to seek Christ.

To this I replied that it was a question of numbers, that the district with a residence should fluctuate between three and five thousand inhabitants at the very most: with this limited number, it seemed to me that the material services rendered would remain the basis for direct human contacts, and would indeed play the same rôle as the matter of the sacraments plays in the transmission of grace.

Our last encounters were with Madeleine D—— and her friends. There we felt truly at home, surrounded by a joy, charity, simplicity recalling St. Clare and the first Franciscans: joy, poverty, charity, total detachment, submission to the circumstances of their lives and the duties of their state, all were harmonised in the community life by M. D—— and her companions, by sheer force of patience and will.

So much for our experiences in Paris. They can be summed up by saying that:

1. Negatively, they reinforced the distrust felt by Marie, and still more by Marguerite, of the too elaborately organised residence.

2. Positively, they inspired in us the desire for a missionary apostolate exercised through the testimony of a life based on the Gospels.

The Residence, consequently, was no longer simply the most perfect expression of mutual aid and social service, it was now also the very form and setting of the missionary life.

At Marseilles, a building had been discovered during the evacuations, when we were helping a neighbour to find somewhere to shelter: a large, converted shop with back-kitchen and sitting-room. Before moving in, we had three days' discussion, so that we could all come to an agreement—Mady, Marguerite, Marie and Anne-Marie.

In the end, we settled on the following formula in an attempt to unite in practice two features which were, in our thought, inseparable:

1. A life shared in all respects with that of the district: before you can be a "good neighbour" you must first be a neighbour, in the same manner as Father de Foucauld in the midst of the Touaregs. For their sake, he led a life of poverty in which personal labour played an important part, so as to share the life of the poor and to remain on intimate and equal terms with them in daily life where one receives in the measure that one gives.

2. The organisation of a centre for material services, in order gradually to improve social conditions and raise the standard of living: the choice of the moment ripe for this establishment depended on the possibility of introducing it into the district without causing too great a shock there, and, above all, without the residents becoming separated from the district itself.

The combination of these two elements was, so to say, both the trademark of the Marseilles enterprise and its sign of contradiction; each of us having to stress one or the other aspect of the Residence every time any difficulty arose.

c

Since I am trying in these lines to record the stages both in the development of the Residence and in the development of my own thought, I include some notes in which I took stock of the position at the end of 1944:

1. Original idea: district establishment run by social assistants or other competent persons, receiving a normal salary. It was almost certain that only girls deeply imbued with the love of Christ would take on this task.

2. Lack of assistants, due to the great self-sacrifice involved: the renunciation, in fact, of all leisure outside the ordinary hours of work. In a job of this kind, one has never finished.

3. But the existence, nevertheless, of girls whole-heartedly desiring to do this work, fully alive to the profoundly wretched circumstances of the lives of the poor and the working-classes. Their ideal: Father de Foucauld, as I have just described him. Hence a life in all respects like that of the people of the district, poor, labouring, etc.

For my part, I continue to believe that there is no need to abandon the idea of the district institution, that on the contrary it will find here complete realisation—but vocations must spring up, not so much among official social assistants as among ordinary girls who wish to give themselves to Christ and the working-class.

Residence.

1. Spontaneous and all-embracing nature of charity.

2. Institution organising a district (and re-creating the temporal parish). This building must also be the "town hall". It will derive its characteristic note not only from the care of the sick (plenty of others do that), assistance in emergencies, planning of leisure, etc., but from the fact that it

has become an essential part of the neighbourhood (where the parish will once more take on body and life). It must be the *heart* of the community, not only because of the tender, fraternal charity that it will embody, but because everything that makes for solidarity in a neighbourhood will nourish it and be in turn nourished by it, like the blood which is pumped by the heart through the whole body. Or again, just as form makes inorganic matter into a specific being with its own inner unity and constitution, so also the Residence. At the present moment, district and parish are alike corpses: the Residence must bring them back to life.

On the 14th of January, Marguerite and Marie, assisted by Anne-Marie, installed themselves in the midst of this world of joy and tears, heroism and poverty.

The contact is real, beneficial, in the true spirit of the Gospel. If there is a wedding or a family party, *les demoiselles* are welcome guests because they are never bored and because they bring an atmosphere of gaiety to the proceedings which would otherwise be lacking.

If you are ill, they come running at the very first call, like mothers and daughters rolled into one: having administered the injection or revived the faint by dint of ringing slaps on the face, they hug you to make up for hurting you.

The local boys' gang have made the Residence their headquarters, because there they are happier, more at peace with the world than anywhere else.

How many ills have been treated, wounds dressed, scalps de-loused, at the Residence, and always in an affectionate, homely atmosphere. It would be easy to go into detail, but the important thing is not so much what is done as the way of doing it, something which is much harder to convey.

Renewed human contacts, Christian hospitality, the fact of being permanently on the spot and completely accessible, these are the essential features of the Residence.

Good cheer, consolation, comfort, these are the first benefits that the Residence procures for those who make use of it.

The duties will be multifarious; no matter!

Sickness to care for, difficulties to straighten out, official forms to obtain, various authorities to approach, children's education to supervise, etc.   Indeed, it seems that the feature which best characterises the Residence is precisely this multitude of direct services answering to individual requests and needs, without any preconceived plan. Even on the level of material assistance, there is no fixed rule, except to promote each person's welfare according to the needs and possibilities of the moment.

But the Residence has a further purpose: it must become a centre of social life in order gradually to raise the standard of living in the neighbourhood; to educate it. But this will be education from within, by unobtrusive influence rather than by set lessons. It must end by becoming organically one with the district of which it aspires to be both head and heart. It has a social function.

This was brought home to me keenly during the liberation battles: that critical period saw the disappearance of all organisations which were not part and parcel of the locality they served. On the other hand, for some fifteen days the girls of the Residence proved the extent to which a service "on the spot" is capable of instant adjustment to the most unforeseen needs.

A network of spontaneous goodwill surrounded them, stretching from the most high-born young socialite down to the lowliest barmaid.

A first-aid station was set up in the shelter where the three to four thousand inhabitants of the immediate environs had taken refuge. It was then that one realised the need for combining technical skill with simple, brotherly friendship. The assistance of a highly competent nurse who happened to be with us at the time was infinitely helpful, and gave everyone a great feeling of security.

At the last moment, in the space of half an hour, the Germans empty the shelters in an attempt to save themselves. We have to set off in the midst of the bombing towards the town, leaving the Residence and everything connected with it behind.

Each of the three girls takes the head of a column: the fearfulness of all these refugees is overwhelming, yet no one has the sense of being utterly lost, because they can still say: "Mademoiselle Marie, where are we going?" "Mademoiselle Berthe, what are we doing?" "Mademoiselle Marguerite, what shall I bring for the baby?"

Thus at every moment of life, crucial or humdrum, this organic solidarity operates. To it working-class poverty and the evangelical life both bring their own special stamp.

Every day the Gospel is increasingly seen as a practical rule of life, more flexible, more detailed and incomparably more liberating than a religious constitution or rule.

As for working-class poverty, it is not synonymous with religious poverty. It is at the same time more organic and less self-conscious; less a matter of working out the extent of one's possessions or the lack of them, than of sharing one's neighbours' lives, and doing nothing that they don't do themselves—and that is saying quite a lot when one is living in a poor district, faced with the problems of food, accommodation, etc.

The proletariat has the poverty of the grasshopper, but it is determined at all costs to avoid the poverty of the ant. In other words, in view of the general instability of things, its chief concern is never to become inextricably committed to any one way of life.

Consequently, vivified by the Gospel and by poverty, this material and moral help bears its full fruit—for it comes from within: it is no longer "good works", it has become mutual help. With the minimum of means one obtains magnificent results.

Madame Bernard is a neighbour of the Residence. She has eight children, each one finer, fatter, dirtier and untidier than the one before. Their clothes are in rags, their scalps highly questionable, but at least they have never known what it feels like to be hungry. She has a husband who has never done much, except give her children; for some years he has had tuberculosis. It is obvious that Madame Bernard cannot live on her unaided resources. Her three elder sons aren't much help, and the swarm of five little ones is a heavy burden.

Moreover, all the social assistants in Marseilles know the Bernard family only too well, every one of them having at one time or another been concerned with it. In spite of help from here, help from there, Madame Bernard cannot manage to make ends meet. So she sings in the streets: one child on the pavement on the right, another on the left, herself in the middle with the third child on her arm (and another soon to come into the world). These street rounds are not much fun either for her or the children, but what is she to do?

One week, catastrophe: in the space of two days she meets the Assistant Chief of Police and the Assistant Chief Justice, two very dictatorial women indeed. They lecture her: "You don't have to be told, you know very well that street-

singing is forbidden when the children are of school age.
You're perfectly well aware it's not allowed . . ."

"Ah, dear lady, if you only do what you're allowed to
these days . . ."

Be that as it may, Madame Bernard is in a really tough
spot. In desperation, she goes and sees her neighbours at the
Residence—well, what all the social workers in the past ten
years have failed to bring about, because they were not
living on the spot, has suddenly become possible.

Prompted by fear of losing this new assistance, vigorous
resolutions are formed: there will be no more singing during
class hours, and the children will go to school. To make
doubly sure, every morning they will report at the Residence
before setting off, and return there in the evening to do their
homework.

In three months the family is transformed. The unedu-
cated children turn out to be very gifted. Madame Bernard
receives no more material aid than she did before, but she
has found something better: fraternal and hard-working
hands to help her, and affectionate hearts to encourage her
to keep going.

CHAPTER V

Missionary Apostolate or Parochial Ministry?

FOR NEARLY two years I have been sharing, to the best of my ability, the lot of my neighbours. I am well aware, however, of all the deficiencies of this apostolate. Too often I am forced to absent myself, for I am continually harassed by these precious social reforms which are, nevertheless, so evidently necessary; the ideal of a life completely merged with that of my neighbours suffers accordingly.

At each absence, even if it is only for three days or a week, I feel on my return that the fraternal bond has slackened. Even if it only takes ten minutes, we have to make each other's acquaintance again. On my side—through a cowardice of which I am ashamed—each time I find returning to the district difficult. How much simpler it is to live in one's monastic cell! In any case, it is not material difficulties that I fear. I know very well that I shall have scarcely reached the bottom of the street when—seeing the children throw themselves into my arms, the women and men show their joy at my return—my apprehensions will vanish. But what is so painful, especially when one lives alone, is to feel oneself torn by the confidences and sorrows of all. When you are living a life where there are no defences up between you and your fellow-beings, each one comes to claim, as it were, a little bit of your heart.

For some time now, I have had a companion, a brother in religion who quickly identified himself with the life of the courtyard. What comfort it is to be no longer alone! Even the weight of sorrow seems eased a little, and just to be able to chat for three minutes before going to bed changes the whole atmosphere.

My companion goes to work on the docks; he is to be seen alternately in white habit and working overalls. This causes no surprise. A neighbour explains to the others: "You see, the little Father [thus they distinguish him from me] has finished his studies and now he wants to go to work so he can understand the troubles of the poor."

Benefiting by the generous privileges granted during the hostilities, this priest has obtained permission from the bishop to celebrate Mass at night. I had already celebrated Mass on several occasions in my room. When we foresaw too big a crowd, we put the bed and stove out in the yard, and on the table where we usually had supper—the Antoine family, my neighbours and myself—the celebration of the Lord's Supper took place.

At the Elevation the Host almost touched the ceiling, but how it shone into the hearts of all those there! Whether they willed it or not, how near they all felt to the Lord Jesus of the Gospel.

It seems that in many minds respect for God and for holy things is proportionate to their remoteness and to the distance in feet that separates them from the faithful. As if in olden days it were better to see Christ from afar than to touch the hem of His cloak!

Why should there be less reverence and recollection because one is nearer to the Master?

But I never celebrated my Mass as regularly as my companion, for in the morning before going to work it is simply not possible. Now, however, some neighbours come every evening, and now and then those who, for one reason or another, feel unworthy to assist at Mass, are represented by flowers bought specially for that purpose—lovely, genuine flowers from the florist. But more beautiful than any flowers are the careful, if heavy, genuflections of this priest who has been working all day on the docks, and whose movements evidence the weights he has been carrying.

The mystery of the Redemption is fulfilled in the very place where it is most needed.

Outside, the seven children of the Vales family play, and when, after our Thanksgiving, we find ourselves back in the yard—all hung with drying laundry and old bedclothes being aired—life seems new to everyone.

In the evening, after supper, between visits from the neighbours, there is catechism and prayer, prayer which gathers up all the trifling events of the day, the joys and troubles of this district of workers.

Each expresses his soul in his own way, for everyone takes part. They all know that one doesn't come in order to please the priest or in the hope of getting some favour from him. In two years, many people have asked me favours of the kind that take place between neighbours; I have often lent money. But no one has ever come to me with a tall story in an attempt to take me in or wheedle money out of me.

Marinette is the first little neighbour with whom I entered into conversation in the very first days of my settling here. Successive evacuations have left us still neighbours. She is one of those who come to prayer. One evening, she doesn't step over the threshold but remains outside.

"You're not coming in, Marinette?"

"No, Father, I've had a row with Juliette and I don't want to forgive her. So I can't say 'Forgive us our trespasses' . . ."

Three days later, the two reconciled belligerents come to pray together.

At the end of the room is a fine poster by a Hungarian artist:

> God is our Father
> We are all brothers
> Let us love one another.

I know that after the first moment or so each of my visitors glances at it; a short silence, a reflection: "Very true . . . if we loved one another. . . ."

Yes, this life is worth while. It bears fruit. To be in the very heart of a mission, you don't have to set out for the Cameroons; you have only to walk across the Coudrère.

Yes, the radiance of the priest's presence spreads through the courtyards and the surrounding alleys. In the stock phrase: "Ah, if all priests were like you . . . " (for which I have the similarly stock retort: "Do you know enough priests to make comparisons?") there is an implied avowal which is not to be lightly ignored.

A life lived in the midst of the most insignificant, the poorest, the humblest, the most abandoned, the most sinful, is a testimony to the plain teaching of the Gospel. When I am waiting for a tram and a strange worker gives me a hostile stare—Good lord, a priest!—he is quite put out when he sees that the people who come up and chat to me cheerfully, like old friends, are the most proletarian of the lot, and that in this case it's he, the one who eyes me askance, who is the bourgeois.

All that is true, and yet the Church, I am forced to admit, makes little impression.

Certainly, these people at least have a parish priest who is not a money-grubber, nor an idler, nor a kind of super-undertaker, nor a capitalist, nor a tool of the employers; but is that so of the rest? Of the Church as a whole?

When my neighbours go to the parish church for one reason or another, they find there a holy priest (I do not say this for politeness' sake but because it is the truth), but they find no parish community to welcome them, and they feel like strangers in the church. The profound tragedy is that the priest is as lonely as they are, but that none of these Christian solitudes succeed in coming together.

When I celebrate Mass in my room or in a special chapel, my neighbours feel perfectly at home, but when they go along to the church for the most important actions of their lives, they find themselves confronted with an administration—even when it comes to "administering" the sacraments. And yet the big parish church retains for them a sure appeal which brings them together there in large crowds.

Every day I appreciate more fully the truth of an objection which the Abbé Godin put to me in the course of one of our conversations: "In your little corner, you will reach a hundred, perhaps two hundred, persons or families, but what about the others? How many priests would we need for three to five thousand people if we are going to live in these conditions?"

Perhaps this objection sounds surprising on the lips of the Abbé Godin, and yet in his view it was conclusive. Admittedly, after his death the priests of the Mission de Paris have also settled in the very midst of the poor, without stopping to ask themselves how many people they would benefit. Do they not seem to fall under the Abbé's criticism? Besides, he himself had lived a life of this kind for several years; but the fact remains that although he had felt the need for personally coming into close contact with the common people, he had proved that this was inadequate as a means of implanting the Church in their midst.

Just now, I am running my head against the same wall. This life that I lead brings me daily treasures, it is an incomparable master of novices: the little that I know I owe to it, and without it I should not even suspect the existence of the problems which confront me. But if it shows me the problems —and this is of enormous value—it does not solve them. Christ founded a Church, a community, a hierarchical community: it is this Church and not a poor little nonentity like myself who must bear witness to Him. Now, this community is, in everyone's eyes, represented by the parish. It is this which must change . . .

Furthermore, a difficulty exists in the provinces which does not arise in Paris. In our cities, fortunately, the parishes —save for rare exceptions—have retained manageable dimensions: eight, twelve, fifteen thousand inhabitants at the most. Now, in a limited area, it is almost impossible, in spite of the utmost good will on the part of the priest of the parish where I was established, and the tact which I try to bring to my own dealings, not to give the people the impression that there are two parallel Churches—that of the proletariat, the little ones, i.e. that of the Gospel; and that of the well-to-do Christian, the demi-bourgeois, i.e. that of the governing class.

In Paris, the co-existence in the same area of a parochial clergy and a missionary clergy does not raise a problem: in these monstrous parishes of sixty or eighty thousand inhabitants any number of missionary groups can live comfortably side by side; rarely will their work interfere with that of the parish clergy. All are alike swamped in the same vast area.

Thus, more and more, is the parish seen to be the great basic reality.

Meanwhile, in my studies and in the works of the *Economie et Humanisme* series, I watched the town-planners and modern architects, French and foreign alike, rediscovering the prime importance of what they called, in their technical language, the "residential unit", the "neighbourhood unit", the "neighbourly or district community". I studied the works of Gaston Bardet, in which he defined the successive stages in the composition of the community, from the group of five or six families, to the city with a population of fifty thousand to a hundred and fifty thousand, every stage revolving around the "parish unit". Here he was joined by the Soviet sociologists, calculating the number of persons which a basic social group should comprise.

Must we, then, at the very time when everyone is returning to the need for organising society into small, regional, basic units, abandon that natural unit which the Church has known throughout the centuries under the name of parish?

Is not the problem, therefore, one of somehow infusing into the district parish all those things which years of missionary experience have proved to be of most value: close personal contact with the people, a life firmly interwoven and organically one with theirs, Christian joy with its exuberance and spontaneity, preaching which springs directly from the events of daily life . . .? This is our first task: we must come to the people not primarily as priests, not primarily as Christians, nor even as brothers and friends: our primary task is to live amongst them and win their acceptance as men.

Like everyone else, I know the defects of our present-day parishes. At times I have suffered acutely, blushed for their mediocrity, for their remoteness from real problems, but all this is no reason for abandoning them. Despite all its shortcomings, its infirmities, the occasional indolence of its clergy and still more of its faithful, the parish remains a great force. This sleeping beauty must be roused.

Admittedly, it adds a heavy load to the missionary task,

with its catechism classes, burial services, its ceremonies at fixed times; but what possibilities of contact it offers, thanks to these very duties. Whether one wishes it or not, the parish is everywhere regarded as the symbol of the Church, and if we cannot succeed in restoring its youth, its joy, its dynamism, confronted by this failure all other efforts will come to nothing. Such a task requires the co-operation of all. It demands that the secular and regular clergy should agree to work together in a common area.

To found an order or a religious congregation would, it seems to me, be a mistake, and certainly experience shows that if the ancient orders have sometimes taken centuries to lose their original flexibility, a few decades have sufficed for this in the case of certain recent orders.

The priests' associations or third orders are, more often than not, hopelessly feeble, and no amount of common devotion to some great priestly model—a saint or the Lord Himself—is going to galvanise them into life. It is not to the past but to the future that they must turn their common gaze, direct their united action.

They must aim at action, but action so far-reaching that we need not fear to call it revolutionary, although in the sense in which Péguy understands the word: "A summons from a less perfect tradition to a more perfect tradition, a summons from a less profound tradition to a more profound tradition, a progression in depth, a quest for deeper sources in the literal sense of re-sources."

In short, it is not a question of founding orders or associations, but of setting in motion the entire clergy as a whole. The chaplains of the Workers' Mission of Paris introduced the idea as far back as 1941:

"The point is to initiate movement. What use is the crew if the ship stays in port? Movement, i.e. a current of activity

directed towards the winning of the masses, and the transformation of our priestly life by the peculiar requirements
of a ministry which is, in part, new; movement which assumes
in the members of the groups which constitute it an unlimited
loyalty, overflowing the juridical bounds of the organisation,
requiring a fusion of minds, expressing itself not only in the
most scrupulous obedience to the duties of the priestly state
and the utmost devotion to the ministry entrusted to us by
the bishop, but also in a sensitive realisation by all of present-
day apostolic problems"; a movement which does not
by-pass the existing organisation, but which, resulting from
a common rediscovery of conditions of life among the masses,
transforms this life in transforming the milieu of the parish.
In other words, a transformation of the priesthood, which,
in the service of the laity, will transform the working-class.

These ideas have long been familiar to the innumerable
groups in which we young priests, both secular and regular,
periodically keep in touch with each other. In one such
group we come together every second Monday for discussion
and prayer, sharing out our difficulties no less readily than
the contributions we bring for supper. But dispersed as we
are over an immense city, how can we effectively work
together?

At all events, we are ready. Our bishop has known all
about the various experiments of the missionary apostolate
from their first tentative beginnings. He has followed every
endeavour, both for social reform in general and for the
reform of life in the immediate neighbourhood. He has
been approached by young people burning to undertake
some such apostolate.

We wait. . . . No doubt the moment is not ripe. All at
once, things happen in a rush. One of us is entrusted with a
parish so that together we may work there as a team.

After that, everything moves terribly quickly. . . . One almost feels like crying halt or asking the bishop for a respite. On the Feast of Christ the King, the head of our group is installed as parish priest.

It is too soon to discuss this parish missionary team. It cannot be seen in proper perspective. But the endeavours of several years have reached their conclusion: our boats are burnt: Christians engaged in social reform, Christians engaged in district planning, a priestly working-team, a new form of mission is born.

The facts which this mission has discovered do not, we are fully aware, carry with them all their solutions, but the union of our mission and its discoveries with the other missions and other like discoveries in Paris, Lisieux or Colombes, fills us with tremendous hope.

PART TWO

CHAPTER VI

The Proletariat and Urban Life

I HAVE retraced the story of the missionary effort pursued at Marseilles and noted its principal stages in order that, drawing from the facts themselves, I might one by one mark off the definite conclusions reached.

What emerges? First the necessity for regarding man not under this or that aspect, but in the totality of his life, good and bad alike. In this way one keeps well clear of sterile discussions on the different activities of this apostolate or their order of importance.

Then comes the need for adopting a way of life which will bring back the healthy members of the community, and particularly Christians, both clergy and faithful, into the main stream of human life. Obviously that does not mean that we invite them to swim with the tide; often they will have to struggle against it; but that is immaterial, the great thing is to be where the stream flows strongest. Next, the need for sharing the troubles and anxieties of work, the injustices of the labour-contract system, living with the workers and their families, finding again the unstudied, simple, happy, brotherly relationships which are the charm and the lesson of the Gospel.

But at the same time it is clear that we must provide action at the required depth, seeking to understand, to dissect the evil, to discern its causes, so as to apply the remedy, not to each sick growth, but to the very root of the disorder which afflicts body and soul. Otherwise our apostolate will be always outstripped by the facts, and will remain perpetually at the stage of the bent-pin fisherman, the stage of ineffectual sighing.

If, then, we want to define concisely what services must be assumed by the missionary apostolate as a whole, how much is to be given to the claims of friendship, how much to preaching the Gospel, how much to spontaneity and how much to organisation, if we want, in the happy comparison of Canon Tiberghien, "neither to fish with a line, nor fish with a net, but to change the water in the pond", we must begin by analysing as accurately as possible the essential features characterising the great urban centres and their repercussions on the lives of the men and families living there.

In the big modern city, man is lost. Anonymous workhand, nameless inhabitant of an area lacking both organisation and local character, he has lost all natural protection. Whereas a fruit or a seed is protected by layers of skin or husk, man no longer has any protective covering at all. Crushed by the hundreds upon thousands of men who surround him, he can find neither help nor protection from them, still less affection or love.

Think of the crowd which sometimes packs into a small space during a popular demonstration. Unlucky the man who happens to be caught there with two or three children; as likely as not father and children will be smothered, knocked down, trampled underfoot. Even the strongest man is in for a bad time if panic breaks out. . . .

Now this is one of the similes which most aptly reflect the urban existence of individuals or families, with no other protection for the person than the coat on his back and the four brick walls—too often miserably cramped—in which he lives. This is the plight of the proletariat: this shattering and dislocation of milieux and natural boundaries which, interlocking one with another, had so effectively protected man and softened the impact of the outside world.

These milieux were the family—not only father, mother and the youngsters—but relatives, brothers and sisters and a whole series of uncles and aunts and cousins, more or less gravitating around a family homestead; the hamlet or district with its friends, its dialect, its customs, its parish; and again, the people of the same calling with their own characteristic trade jargon. All these milieux were sources of life: man took root in them like a tree which finds, at different depths, the earth and water necessary to its life, and ultimately the rock to which it clings.

The minimum protection afforded by food and clothing was thus immeasurably extended in these social groupings. Between man and nation, between man and humanity intervened a whole series of protective layers. This, allowing for more or less deficient realisations, was well on the way to being universal, as is evidenced by the Christianity of the Middle Ages when, for instance, a common spiritual and intellectual sap united Paris and Helsinki. But it is not necessary to go back to the Middle Ages: these protective sheaths have persisted wherever society has remained predominantly rural and the towns of small dimensions.

But when the towns swelled, when each year they collected tens of thousands of national and foreign immigrants, man found himself alone. He endeavoured to form fresh groups, sometimes on the basis of common nationality—particularly if he came from afar, e.g. the Poles, Armenians, North Africans, Spaniards and Italians, who tend to form little communities of streets or blocks of houses. But this is the exception, and even here man finds no stable context, but is delivered up defenceless to the dense masses of urban life.

Fruit and vegetables are handled in cases or baskets, each fruit separated from the others by straw or a twist of paper, so that there is no chance of their spoiling. But man lives in bulk like loose produce, coal, turnips, phosphates—flattened, compressed, smothered, crushed by the weight of all his fellow-beings.

It is in the working-class world that man has suffered this oppression most grievously, because here it has been increased twofold by the most flagrant form of exploitation. Consequently, it is here that men first thought of combining and protecting themselves by forming associations. The trade unions thus represent the first efforts to escape from anonymity by endeavouring to make their members politically conscious and *organised* citizens. This word "organised" has sometimes provoked a smile but is none the less deeply significant.

But this effort, despite the immense amount already undertaken and achieved, has failed to change the social climate. In the end, we are still left with a profit-run society. Let us be quite clear on this point: the insecurity and instability of the working-class have not been abolished.

The labourer and his family are never sure of the next day: many do not know whether or not the following half-day will find them out of work; all, even the highly qualified, are at the mercy not only of the great political cataclysms but of a thousand other contingencies as well: unemployment, sickness, economic crises, shifts in the labour exchange or in international markets, changes in fashion, bad labour organisation, etc.

In these conditions, it is impossible to make either short or long-term forecasts: a striking example is provided by the workers' tenements where numbers of families all crowd in together, since they can none of them count on being able, three or six months hence, to pay a decent rent. Also, all money is spent on food (and amusements, if there is any over) : the very notion of saving has, inevitably, lost all meaning: the bottomless cask of the daughters of Danaus is the myth which most accurately sums up modern working-class life. Wages are spent from day to day, almost the moment they are earned.

One actual happening will sufficiently illustrate the point: a rag-and-bone dealer making his way to his hut fell down a ninety-foot drop and was killed—his hut, as it happened, was built on one of the hills overlooking the town: to reach it he had to cross a kind of path along the ledge of the town wall, so narrow that one could only go round very cautiously, step by step. The least slip, the least inadvertence, which on an ordinary path would not matter in the slightest, here meant a somersault to death.

Here is a "real life" symbol of the life of the working-classes, where everything is so finely adjusted, so uncertainly balanced, that the tiniest error, the least bit of bad luck, the least mistake, result in an irrevocable fall. A man may be a qualified workman; he drops to docker, then collier. Within this latter grade there still remains a whole gamut of downfalls to pass through.

Thus, in addition to its insecurity, the manual labour of the workman burdened with a family has a tragic quality of necessity which distinguishes it from all others. As R. Garric has rightly observed, others may have to work harder than the labourer, but they are not, like him, under the law of *immediate* necessity:

"Let us clearly realise the harsh and uncompromising flavour of this word which so strongly characterises

working-class life: we all must work, but for the labourer
absence of work—even temporary—instantly spells want,
dole, hunger.

"How can people understand this if they are not
intimately acquainted with the lives of the working-
classes, if they haven't sat at the common table, if they
haven't shared not only the bread but the troubles and
anguish of each day?"[1]

Agreed, it is good, in fact it is imperative, that man be
enmeshed in a web of necessities: the official who can take a
holiday whenever he pleases is by no means the ideal type
of worker. In fact, the great drawback of numerous leaders'
schools or youth groups has been that the leaders and young
people were not engaged in a real job, where work was
strictly obligatory.

So there is a healthy necessity which sustains a man,
which is for him a vital medium, a protective framework;
but the peculiarity which distinguishes proletarian life is
the *inorganic* nature of this necessity. Gustave Thibon has
summed it up in two vivid words: instead of being both a
goad and a nourishing breast—"*un aiguillon et une mamelle*"
—it is only a goad.

This certainly does not mean that the labourer does not
earn big money at certain times, nor that on certain days
his table isn't better provided than that of the bourgeois.
But always he lives in insecurity.

Hence the proletariat, alternately prospering and suffering
want, goes through life like a motorist with no spare wheel:
the least puncture in one wheel inevitably means total break-
down for all four.

This common and peculiar destiny which oppresses the
labouring masses has marked them off from other groups

[1] *Belle-Ville*, p. 176.

and led to their becoming a separate class, which has been gradually forced into separate districts.

I have stressed the question of living "in bulk", the absence of protective partitions, because it is of such capital importance. It is true that in the course of time certain partitions have sprung up—but invariably for the wrong reasons. Far from *protecting* or *compassing* relatively self-contained groups, they have—for the purpose of avoiding disagreeable contacts—*separated* rich and poor. To the absence of protective milieux is added the separation of people into distinct geographic groups: aristocrats, bourgeois, employers, proletariat, sub-proletariat. Social mixing is a thing of the past: the teacher who instructs you, the doctor who prescribes for you, the priest who absolves you, all come from outside with their services or blessings.

And urban society has all but finally sanctioned this position by the creation of a "zoning" system, distinguishing not only industrial and residential zones, but within the latter a number of different categories.

Thus we come back to the other salient problem of urban life: housing. So much has been said and re-said, written and re-written on this subject, that one apologises for reverting to it. However, I am not going into further descriptions or details here; either you know from your own experience the evils of the slum and the over-crowded tenement, or you don't, in which case all the descriptions in the world are useless. Shelter, which provides for the necessities of rest and procreation, is, after food and clothing, the third essential need of man. So long as the housing question remains at its present stage, all effort towards reconstruction or regeneration in no matter what field will certainly fail. And it is not solely a matter of ensuring the essential minimum of space and comfort (shower-rooms, heating, etc.), but also of providing education—teaching people to be good tenants, while at the same time we plan their future homes.

England has seen the birth of a new social function: the director of municipal housing instructs the people in his locality in hygiene and in the art of being good neighbours.

Anonymity and insecurity, isolation from the educative influence of other environments and the absence of protective groups, have an injurious effect on children for which nothing, or almost nothing, can compensate; it is these factors which are responsible for the appalling circumstances in which so many children are being brought up—or, if you like, dragged up. They are no longer, strictly speaking, brought up, educated. The social milieu being non-existent and the family too oppressed to function as it should, the child—lacking all natural defence—grows like a wild plant, passing from the sun of its own good pleasure and the "let the kid do as he likes if it keeps him happy", to the tempest of blows and kicks.

Ever since he was born, his body has known neither discipline nor training. He has sucked, eaten, cried, slept, relieved himself, demanded or refused his dummy when and as he wished. From the first weeks of his life, his body has been developing into a tyrant which sooner or later gains complete control of him. As a baby, he was carried around for months, sometimes years, to prevent him from crying, and his eldest sister had to stay away from school "because of baby".

What is the weft on which the young worker's mentality is woven? You will have to unravel a whole series of layers and sheaths to find this lad of fourteen, who looks on himself as a man from the day he got into long trousers and started earning wages.

His education has been undertaken by everyone and no

one: school, very little; family, also very little; more by the
street, his pals, the bar; most of all by the cinema. Those
who are educated are those who have the *certificat d'études*;
only a tiny minority can write; at the age of fourteen the
majority are illiterate or quickly lapse into illiteracy. Geo-
graphy and history they all know purely from the films.
"Yes, it's true, I saw it in Ben Hur", declares a lad to two
others who are discussing the sufferings of the ancients; or
again: "I couldn't make head or tail of the newspapers if
I didn't see the newsreels."

This education is at the bottom of their curious mixture of
dishonesty and a very genuine scrupulousness; the joy and
pride in their work in the first few months of the job are soon
replaced by deliberate inefficiency "so as not to line the
boss's pocket". This is sufficient justification, so far as they
are concerned, for renouncing everything that would raise
the standard of their lives, yet at the same time they tell
their young brother to go to school and make something
of himself, and never become "a bad egg like me".

Grafted onto this random education is a sickening famili-
arity with life seen from below: a week after starting the job,
the young boys are introduced, by the men and married
women, to realities which, great in themselves, are inex-
pressibly debased in their presentation. At twelve years of
age for a good many, at fourteen or sixteen for the majority,
there is nothing that they do not know about the sexual life.
Absolutely intoxicated by the discovery of physical love, they
visit prostitutes and brothels regularly. Even apart from the
pleasure that they seek there, a fresh set of bad influences
duly leaves its mark on them, since they are inevitably
affected by the whole atmosphere of these places.

But afterwards comes the melancholy of the young man
who thinks that life has nothing more to offer, who feels that

he has reached the summit. What happens to other men at thirty-five, forty, fifty, comes to him at sixteen or eighteen. So far as the rest of his life is concerned, he's "had it". The will is deadened, and if it does try to assert itself it is less for the sake of being, say, more expert or efficient at a particular job, than of appearing so. He wants to be "tough", and has no time for terms of affection if he suspects that they are a sign of "softness" or inferiority.

This, together with the cap pulled over one eye, the flash tie for Sundays and the cigarette—what are they, save the desires of a thwarted virility which has missed its proper (in all senses of the word) field of expression and declares itself in outward symbols?

Only the best will seek in Communism or Christianity a sublimation, a *mystique*: they will be the militants. The others will bring with them all the secret resentment of their frustrated lives. Founding a home of their own will be the last hope, but for the vast majority the accumulation of so many bad habits, so many disappointments and disillusions makes it all but impossible for any spark of love, even sincere love, to kindle their lives.

Is the young working woman in any better case? Hardly. At fourteen the little girl starts her working life. She takes the first job that offers without dreaming of consulting her own tastes or aspirations. Here again the necessities of life and the needs of the family are the over-riding considerations.

As an apprentice, she runs all the workroom errands, does the proprietress's shopping, stands in queues, even exercises the dog. If she cannot stand up for herself, she is the butt of all and sundry, until such time as another takes her place. It is seldom that she is able to practise her trade. In order to get on she would have to change her job, but she rarely acts independently in this first period, which lasts from one and a half to two years.

Psychologically and morally, she, too, duly comes up against the hyper-sexualised atmosphere of the workroom. Two days suffice at the factory to "open a kid's eyes". In the workroom they are more sophisticated in their methods, one might even say tactful, but the resulting distress and shock are no less keen.

Some girls withdraw into themselves at this stage, others let themselves go, and soon—in the excitement of the first make-up and the desire to be in the swim—become friendly with any young man who will take them to the pictures and pay for their various little fads and fancies.

In certain environments, to remain decent means to be heroic.

Some who possess the *certificat d'études* by way of intellectual assets and who wish to get on, attend evening classes—but at what a cost: leaving the workroom at seven o'clock, going to the class at seven-thirty to eight-thirty, coming home at nine for supper, tidying the kitchen for the next day, mending and pressing clothes and going to bed at midnight or one o'clock.

For a great number, the home with its housework, kitchen chores, washing and scrubbing—so ruinous to the hands— amounts to a second day's work, additionally tedious in proportion to the lack of domestic amenities.

Comparing girls and boys, it may be said that the boys as a whole tend to remain in the same mediocre rut, the girls to separate into two groups: a small minority, generally coming from large families, remarkable for their unselfishness and affection, teachers in the true sense of the word; and a great majority without anything much in their heads at all.

Among the latter, motherhood will be a remedy in some cases, but very few are properly prepared for it.

Thus boys and girls alike start out in life without any trade or technical training, and, more important, without character or will. It is by no means their fault; where could they acquire these things? So the dilemma often seems reduced to this: either to leave the children to families unfit for their task, to be reared in hovels amidst squalor, neglect and insecurity, or to take them away from their families, which is tantamount to breaking the sole bond which unites the child to its rich, natural soil, and so preparing generations of quasi-orphans.

One solution alone escapes the dilemma: to leave children in their families—save those manifestly unworthy of the charge—but to help the family to secure everything which it must normally be able to provide in fulfilling its function.

This precarious and rootless existence of the working-class family has resulted in the setting up of a *Service Social*. It was with the genuine intention of helping the family—which entailed personal supervision of the education of children, the housing improvements, etc., which it wished to promote —that the *Service Social* laboured during its first years, with all the greater understanding where it was directed by thoroughly experienced women dedicated to the cause of the masses.

Now today, the *Service Social* is often recognised to be largely ineffective. Why?

First, because it has lost touch with the families; right in its initial stages, the *Service Social* developed into an enterprise, abandoning its former regional organisation based on the service of small local areas. It had started with visiting nurses for children, who attended private homes in a given district or zone. It was then in the nature of a health service.

Certain industrial concerns, impressed by its benefits, had co-opted it, but in essence it remained unchanged.

Then, after having revolved for a time around these big factories, it made them its headquarters: abandoning the working-class family and its natural setting, the home, it turned its attention to the labourer in *his* natural setting, the factory. And so, ultimately, was born the factory welfare officer. Indicative of the present situation is this remark, made to certain of these officials by an inspector responsible for giving them their directives: "Ladies, there are still too many of you who go out visiting families." How many, among the new generation of social workers, have preserved intimate contact with the family? Investigation permits me to say that there are fewer and fewer.

After this, the *Service Social* became too bureaucratic, too centralised. Enquiries, forms to be filled in, questionnaires multiply indefinitely, to the detriment of true human contacts. It controls rather than consoles, issues instructions rather than educates. Because it is associated with the employer or a public department, people distrust it. After all, they can scarcely be expected to trust a thing which enters their life without warning, and which depends for its existence on those whom they like least and whom they have most reason to suspect of prying into their affairs: the employer and the State.

Consequently, in present-day society, man, or more precisely the family, is cut into sections. Society is no longer treated as a single entity. Hence we see an extensive series of social services spring up, each dealing with only one aspect of the whole: mothers' clubs, clubs for the unemployed, prisoners' clubs, etc. Granted that each corresponds to a need, it still remains true that none is concerned with the whole man in his ordinary daily environment.

Furthermore, since their relief measures involve drafting people into various types of institution, the welfare services tend to break up the family at its very core: the boy in an apprenticeship school, the girl in a sanatorium, the baby at the crèche, grandmother in an institute for the aged; who is left in the home? In certain cases, perhaps, such measures are inevitable, but they should only be resorted to when it is quite clear that no other solution is possible. But precisely to the extent that the *Service Social* works from the outside, it is hard to see what other methods it could use. Consequently, because it acts from without and in a disjointed manner—both in space and time—the *Service Social* can only do its best to ameliorate the evils brought to its notice, and then only after these evils have taken firm hold. It seldom has a preventive function. It tackles the evil in its multiple effects at the cost of great self-sacrifice and unwearying patience on the part of the assistants. But it fails to stamp out the cause of the evil. It fails to improve the general condition of the sickness, curing at one stroke all its multiple infirmities.

Finally, it finds it difficult to develop into an educative force, owing to lack of time and inability to be constantly on the spot. The gravest obstacle in this respect is the employment of interchangeable visiting welfare officers, who generally have no special link with the district and no permanent establishment. The more these social services are multiplied (with all their inherent administrative formalities) the more cut off the people will feel, the deeper will be the gulf between those who give and those who receive.

"The example of a certain political party before the war is conclusive evidence. Its endeavours—based strictly on a programme of social charities—only succeeded in incurring the ingratitude of the masses and in increasing bourgeois solidarity.

"This is easily accounted for. Beneficence galls the beneficiary. It excites an outburst of good fellowship only among those who are doing the giving or the helping, those who are making the sacrifices. Hence the failure of this party's charitable projects in the working-class milieux (the receiving end) and their success in the bourgeois milieux (the giving and self-sacrificing end).

"The same reasons explain the success of the Marxist parties. Their charitable projects were included in the great movement for social reorganisation which they advocated. Charity lost its patronising character and became an element in the construction of the future city. Henceforward, charities were regarded as an integral part of the revolutionary programme."[1]

The Greeks loved speaking of "day-togethering" as a characteristic of friendship: living together through the day; being happy together, unhappy together—and it is this alone which can break down the hostile barriers described by St. Paul.

The classical example is the olden-time village: when the hail came down, all the peasants were alike affected, and they lamented together. But there was one whose groans rose louder than the rest: this was the merchant, for he knew that the peasants could always manage to get enough to eat; but as for him, if the harvest was bad who would buy his goods?

Thus the storm was an even greater catastrophe for those in the village who possessed no field of their own. But today, so far as the teacher, the welfare worker or even the priest are concerned, it can thunder and hail as much as it likes, they are no less sure of their wages—big or small, it makes no difference—at the end of the month.

[1] From an unpublished document.

D

This is why all analogies and metaphors drawn from the human body are so important when one is thinking of human society. The head and the members are not only the classical image of our *communauté de destin*, but the key which must be applied to every social problem. And a body, conceived as a living being, can only be built up from small cells in direct contact one with another.

Hence if the help which we are eager to render, in whatever form it may be, material or spiritual, is to be welcome and effective, there must always be—if not equality of material conditions—at least the recognition of this *communauté de destin*, and this in turn implies personal presence. The people as a whole, no less than the individual, will never be saved by outside intervention.

This notion of participation in one life, one destiny, is too important to be passed over cursorily. It is the touchstone which enables us to tell whether or not a given social climate is suitable for human habitation, whether social life can thrive in the setting envisaged. It presupposes two things: a certain similitude, a resemblance, but above all an interdependence, an organic solidarity: the first is that which exists between two men of the same social class; the second links, for instance, a sailor and his captain on the same ship.

Now, nearly three years of living in poor districts have convinced me that close identification with the life of the district, and daily and familiar contact with its inhabitants, will enable one "from the inside"—naturally, as it were, and without recourse to artificial means—to set these people on their feet again. If we refuse to be reconciled to the present inhuman ordering of society, we must first make a realistic study of the general conditions of men's lives, in order to see clearly which remedies will be genuinely effective and practically possible; but we must also have instruments to apply these remedies and make them penetrate into the masses. Now, only by installing in the district an organism, living its life and sharing its rhythm, shall we be able to discover with certainty the economic and social conditions—both general conditions and those applicable to special groups—which will restore man to natural, stable milieux (family, district, city, region, trade). Still more, we must not only bring a theoretical solution to these problems, and to the problems of housing, town-planning, education, apprenticeship, leisure, etc., we must proceed to carry them out—and only the permanently established "residence" will be capable of this, for it alone is in touch both with the evils and with the remedies for them. Here, as in philosophy, or, for that matter, anywhere else, "action at a distance repels".

CHAPTER VII

The Proletariat and Religion

IF WE consider only the positive features of urban life, we could stop at this point without so much as mentioning the religious factor, so little real part does it play in the life of the masses. Out of a hundred persons, perhaps ninety are baptised, but only ten make their Easter duty regularly, and only two or three are well-instructed and alive to the implications of their religion. And this average applies to the bourgeois districts. One could not say even this much of a hundred people picked at random in, say, a suburban tram. . . .

In the working-class parishes of fifteen to twenty thousand inhabitants, one thousand at the very most are touched by the Church; these are the sympathisers. Four or five hundred come to Mass on Sundays, say one in forty.

An adult who has passed by this building they call a church every day, perhaps, since his childhood, has never once dreamt of going in. What he would find inside he hasn't the least idea: benches, chairs, a font? He is as ignorant as we might be of a Shintoist temple. . . .

Madame Durain is a baptised Frenchwoman; she is from la Drôme but has always lived in Grenoble or Marseilles; she is forty and has three children. Paulot, the youngest of them, is a boy scout. She attends his induction and the outdoor Mass which accompanies it. After the ceremony, she questions the neighbour who came with her:

"By the way, what was that little tablet the priest gave everyone who knelt down?"

The Host and Communion are explained to her.

"Ah, so that's what Paulot had when he made his First Communion."

When one hears the phrase "I am a Christian", it often means this: "I am a Christian—in other words, a member of the white races, neither Musulman nor Jew; I do not disagree with the Church to the point of refusing to do for my children what my parents did for me; I have kept a vague religiosity."

To be a Christian means "I'm not against it . . ."

The proletariat is a pagan people with Christian superstitions. These superstitions are known as Baptism, First Communion, Marriage, Religious Burial. Why, yes, one would prefer to believe in God rather than to believe, as one does, in nothing at all. But how can one? In church, you hear nothing but the same exhortations, the same old tales in their biblical jargon. Then this Church—where you ought at least to find a fellowship which would deliver you from loneliness and unnatural isolation—apparently leaves you in your loneliness, and actually reinforces the barriers of your isolation with all the weight of its draperies, its candles and its hierarchical structure.

Meanwhile you keep—until the time comes when it dies altogether—a faint nostalgia for God somewhere in your heart. So you are grateful to those who, not by their words but by their lives, give you reason for believing and hoping in Him. But where are they to be met, these people who preach without words?

But we may well ask if these "feelers", as it were, for the supernatural do exist, if there really is a receptiveness for religious emotion, a kind of natural foothold for grace.

At the present time, many militant workers feel very keenly the need for what they call "moral reforms", as a counter to the scandal of prostitution, and the primacy of money-making. But for them the remedy is simple: one merely has to change the government! This is a long way from even the preliminaries to a spiritual approach, and I don't think that it can, properly speaking, be called a "feeler".

Living amidst machinery, they regard the body as a piece of mechanism. When this notion is supplemented by materialist propaganda, they have a sufficient explanation of the universe. They feel that they are helpless units in a blind, inexorable world, and they have no instinctive reactions against this fatal determinism. They aspire solely to change the material conditions of life, breaking the mechanical chain of cause and effect which binds them down, in order that they in their turn may become the beneficiaries of a new system.

These considerations seem pessimistic to some. However, I am not forgetting the great spiritual upheaval which for the last hundred years has been agitating the heart of the working-class movement. The emancipation of the people by its own leaders has given birth to heroes, martyrs, saints.

Re-read the story of the "Chicago martyrs", who in 1887 originated May Day. Take up again the recently published letters of the militants—believers and atheists—shot during the Occupation. We find there much more than "feelers" for the supernatural; we are breathing its very air: "There is no greater love than this, that a man lay down his life for his friends. . . ."

Thus, the most authentic aspirations towards the transcendent, towards a *mystique*, find their expression for *non-Christians* in Communism and syndicalism.

But the achievements of such leaders are rare; the great majority have no part in them and show little evidence of caring much about anything. Sometimes there is a sense of human dignity. When one manages to treat even a member of the sub-proletariat as a man, truly recognising and according him his dignity as a human being, there arises in him a kind of urge towards greater things. He escapes, if only momentarily, from the pitiless oppression of a machine-like existence. He holds up his head. He recovers something of his old faith in himself.

Could the desire for social justice be regarded as a spiritual "feeler"? Unfortunately, I do not think that there is a desire for social justice in the great proletarian masses. There is scarcely more than a vast collective demand, more or less unformulated. The world, humanity—"To hell with them!" The Boches are swine, so are the Americans. There are only the Russians left, and even they shouldn't be looked at too closely.

Do decency and loyalty constitute "feelers"? People have forgotten their existence, so discussion is pointless. Real unselfishness would undoubtedly make some impression on them, but only if they were confronted with it over a long period.

The desire to work for the glory and good of the country provides firmer ground. The Communists have laboured this a good deal. Up to a point it could be a force, but in actual fact I do not think it is. Recent conflicts in a factory in Marseilles have proved that the desire to work for patriotic motives is less strong than the desire to oppose "the boss", and less strong again than the desire to "take it easy".

The common people are more capable of generosity than anyone. Nevertheless, one cannot count on this as a permanent characteristic of the masses (any more than of any other class).

Sickness and poverty? Among people normally indifferent to the supernatural, infinitely more turn against it as a result of sickness and poverty than are led to embrace it.

What is there on the positive side? Real solidarity, profound unselfishness exist in the working classes, this is beyond question. This could constitute a "feeler". But against this is something which strikes one no less forcibly, namely that in this great mass of men, united by the same cruel mechanised existence, there is no tendency to form groups of friends, genuine pals. . . .

Two things remain, like a little flame, however fleeting: the first, love. When, after all the excesses of youth, the young man is about to found a home of his own, a light kindles in his heart. This is the moment when the young are open to higher things. The second goes much deeper: the paternal-filial instinct. When one sees a worker who treasures the memory of his parents, one can be quite sure that here is fit soil for the action of Grace, a firm foundation. But it is imperative that this filial memory be whole and untarnished. If it has been associated with too many quarrels, too much unhappiness, it cannot stand much pressure.

All things considered, then, can one speak of supernatural "feelers" among the people? I believe that the answer must be No. On the contrary, their souls are dimly aware of a great emptiness. But this very emptiness is great cause for hope, for when God sees an empty soul He hastens to fill it, and in such a soul the Gospel will take deep root. So we find nothing positive, simply a void, a void hollowed out in man by hunger and thirst: what theologians would call an "obediential potency".

The apostles who are to bring the Gospel must be truly capable of filling this void.

"Christianity is no longer the leaven which ferments the world," states Père Schulte in *Le Prêtre d'aujourd'hui*. To which we add: it is not that the leaven has lost any of its power, but rather that it is no longer mixed with the dough, and so is unable to act. Despite their acerbity, certain extracts from Père Schulte will help to sum up our conclusions:

"We carry on traditions without asking ourselves if it would not be more useful, these days, to find out whether success attends this outlay of time and energy, and whether perhaps a fundamental change is not required. . . . Here and there, we seem to be at one with those who say, 'The materialistic outlook of the masses will not be transcended until it has evolved to its utmost limit, thus destroying itself'. Priests may contemplate this evolution in all tranquillity. Admittedly, the materialism prevailing in so many milieux will in the end lead men to the abyss. But we would deceive ourselves terribly if we assumed that the masses, like the prodigal son in the parable, will then return penitent and sorrowful to the Church. If we fail to approach the present generation, the future generations who grow up outside the Church's influence will be incomparably more difficult to reach. They will be brought up to hate and scorn everything to do with Church and priesthood. And how could we bear to remain in an attitude of passive expectancy in the face of the religious and moral destitution of so great a number?"

One day, following a lecture by Père Schulte, a man who openly declared himself a Communist leader asked permission to speak. He expressed himself something like this: "If it were possible today to win men to the ideas set forth by the speaker, there would be no need for Communism. We should have social equality then in every class and calling. But do you think," he said, turning to me, "that you are able, with all your speeches and lectures, to change men's outlook today? If a worker and his family were wandering around this town this very night, without means or shelter, do you mean to tell me that out of all your hearers —who call themselves good Catholics and never dream of missing Mass on Sundays—there would be a single one who would be willing to share his home with that family? And if there were, do you suppose people wouldn't mock him for a fool? Can you think of a Christian industrialist, lying snugly under three warm blankets, and hearing these shelterless wretches wandering the streets, who would so much as get out of bed and give them one of his blankets? Certainly you can't, in spite of your lectures. We Communists, we have a mission to fulfil. . . ."

Talking is not enough, we must give the example. The ecclesiastical assistant at Cologne, Monseigneur Stoffels, while walking with a friend, stopped by a block of workers' flats and said sadly, "If we could make up our minds to leave our own fine homes and become workers with the workers, what a different picture we'd present in the eyes of the masses. To them, our way of life smacks too strongly of the capitalist."

Thus from the religious viewpoint, even more than from the economic, it is of the utmost urgency that we should enter into a common life with the masses, a real sharing of their lot.

Disregarding fine distinctions, it seems possible to trace three great periods in the history of the Church.[1]

In the earliest times, the Church, lacking power and influence, was unable to take up any stand on the general social problems then current: turning aside from the field of theory, she nevertheless introduced—through the institution

---

[1] Let us stress, once and for all, that by Church we mean not merely the clergy, but the whole Christian community: a living body does not breathe by its lungs alone, but also by its pores.

of deacons—various charitable services into the daily social life of that time: collections for the poor, hospitality to strangers, to social inferiors, etc. The Catholic epistles, particularly the epistle to Diognetus, are sufficient proof.

Through the mingling of the classes in religious assemblies and at the common meal, living evidence of men's equality before God, the social question was, if not wholly, at least very largely resolved. Imagine, recalling the situation of the slave in ancient Rome, the impression created by the union of the wealthy Roman and those who didn't even own their own bodies, the patrician and the slave—separated by an infinitely wider gulf than today separates a coal-trimmer or coal-heaver from the chief director of a great shipping company—fraternising on equal terms, one in charity, sharing the same faith and the same religious ritual. Where today would you find a fashionable bourgeois and an old-clothes dealer from the slums meeting together, in a spirit not of patronage but of love?

These humble activities multiplied in the Middle Ages: right of asylum, ransoming of captives, construction of bridges, land cultivation, manufacturing—the Carthusians were also ironsmiths—all helped to produce a balance between the economic life of a region and that of its inhabitants. Every convent or ecclesiastical college was at one and the same time an apostolic centre and a centre of civilisation: the cultivation of soil and spirit went hand in hand.

The Church, grown strong and influential, and now able to turn to more general considerations, including questions of social doctrine, felt no less bound to intervene on this level too.

At the present time, the Church enjoys greater authority and power than she ever possessed in her early history; consequently, she has the duty of acting on the general plane:

she cannot, without betrayal, remain "as if she neither saw nor understood",[1] and when she sees that "the Christian life has become practically impossible for the great mass of the people.",[2] she must not hesitate to take up her stand against governments.

But—and here is the whole tragedy—unlike the Church of the Middle Ages, the Church today has lost the affection and the attention of the common people. They, on their side, ask her by what right she claims to interfere with and direct from above the spiritual and moral life of men with whom she is no longer involved in the everyday events of life, the daily task of bread-winning.

Having ceased to fulfil her rôle as nurse and mother, her doctrinal rôle becomes intolerable; this tender mother seems like a strange governess, her charity like condescending alms-giving.

What is the maternal rôle of the Church? What does a mother do for her children? Certainly, she sets aside time to teach them the most sublime truths of heart and soul, but she provides also for the essential and ever-recurring needs of clothing, food and shelter; she watches over the sick-bed, stands between her children and the consequences of their various follies.

It seems desirable then, in fact imperative, that the Church should manifest herself to the people in her true rôle, entering into the entire daily life of the masses, flesh-and-blood workers—not in doctrinal matters alone, but in all the practical details of day-to-day living: labour-contracting, wages, conditions of work, security and stability of employment, sustenance, lodging, etc. She must continue the work of the labouring monks and pioneers of old, but in another sphere.

[1] Pius XII, Pentecost Message, 1941.   [2] Pius XII, ibid.

In thus ensuring that "Providence is placed within reach of the weak and needy", the Church has no thought of taking over governing or administrative functions from the proper authorities; she is simply bent on once more becoming the leaven which, closely mingled with the dough, causes the whole loaf to rise and not merely a few portions destined for the tables of the ruling class or the élite.

The Church has indeed never ceased rendering this material aid: witness her orphanages, welfare centres, crèches, day nurseries, the Little Sisters of the Poor, the nursing orders. But this is precisely the point: the form of these charities has scarcely changed for several centuries, and many others which used to exist have perished through lack of adaptation.

Those which have survived are the peculiarly feminine works of charity, but those formerly the province of knights, bishops, abbots or monks have disappeared: right of asylum, ransom of prisoners, bridge-building, the "Truce of God", the rendering of justice to the poor, strength placed at the service of the oppressed, real and effective protection of the hapless even where it involved defying the ruler of the city; in short, everything which could be called the man's part in the works of mercy has lapsed, owing to failure of adaptation to new human needs.

Would this be a case of unlawful intervention in temporal affairs? No, for it is a question here of helping people in the field of those daily human actions on which their salvation depends. If the Church is bound to teach men detachment from material possessions, she is no less bound to see that all creatures have their place in the created order, with the possession of that vital minimum of personal and domestic property that God has assigned to each, to enable him to accomplish his destiny.

If these premises are granted, what are the practical obstacles which at the present time combine to hinder the civilising influence of the Church and its true apostolate? What constitutes the modern barricade between the people and God?

First and foremost, the conviction that the Church is identified with the rich, the employer class, the powerful, the government. Just as nothing—not all the balance-sheets in the world—will persuade the worker that the firm which employs him doesn't make enormous profits, or move him from his conviction that the whole system needs reorganising, so, too, the people will not believe that the Church is the home of the poor, that it is harder for the rich man to enter heaven than for a camel to go through the eye of a needle, that the first beatitude is that of the poor and the humble. They will never believe this if things do not change, if they do not see the Church welcoming the worker, encouraging, defending, protecting him, if the representatives of the Church do not concern themselves with the texture of his life.

In the eyes of the people, the priest is a man not of life but of death, the man who appears between the hearse and the bosses at big funerals—"chief undertaker's assistant" they say; and indeed the church sacristies, covered with notices and placards recalling the formal and administrative side of the actions of worship, are not calculated to give them any other notion.

Going one day into an alley which I had never previously entered, I met a woman rinsing her washing at the well. As I passed, I read such consternation on her face that I stopped: "Why, what's happened, madam? Has there been an accident?" The answer came in a burst of apprehension: "What have you come here for? Who's dying?"

And here is another testimony: "Priests don't come for the

love of us, they only turn up for burials. They come and bless the body if you give them thirty-five francs—otherwise we don't see them."

Have we still ears to hear to what the common people are saying?

In the South, they call the priest a "sprat-catcher", an expression that one can think about, for it indicates both the mediocrity of the result and the tireless patience of the single-line fisherman, ever hopeful of a bite.

One more definition, recent and authentic: "The priest is the man of money, the middle class, and death, who refuses to lie with a woman, it's hard to know why . . ."

The last point remains a mystery to some, for despite all the gossip and a few sad scandals, they do believe that it is, in fact, so. But there is no trace of doubt in their minds about the first three!

We personally know only too well that young curates—at any rate in the provinces—receive scarcely better salaries than little errand- or office-boys. But when people see the leather armchair in the presbytery, and the housekeeper— even if she happens to be the priest's mother—they promptly take scandal:

"That fellow has a housekeeper and a good salary. He's doing pretty well. . . ."

So the first obstacle to conquer is the fact that in the Church, secular and regular clergy—even when they are personally poor—live in the rhythm of the bourgeois classes: if one is asked with which side their lot is cast, one is forced to reply that it is with the well-to-do, the settled, the respectable classes, and in no sense with the poor, the workers, the proletariat. Even when their poverty is quite genuine, it lacks the dynamic aspect which St. Francis and St. Dominic gave it. The monks no longer look like men who have chosen to be beggars, as was intended by the founders of the great apostolic orders; on the contrary, appearances often support those who reproach the men of the Church with living by bourgeois standards. They have an air of security, stability, of being nicely set up in life, which, whether they wish it or not, separates them too sharply from the workers, who almost all—even the best and the most highly qualified—pass their entire existence in insecurity, instability and uncertainty.

Some nursing nuns settled in the midst of an exclusively working-class population, in a central industrial town. Enthusiastically welcomed, when the first flutter caused by their arrival had died down, they became aware of a certain uneasiness: "Look at the potatoes they get in, and the coal. . . ." they heard people whisper. Yet this was an excellent community, truly self-sacrificing, poor and fervent; but there were twelve of them, and this number necessitated a measure of organisation which, allied to the habitual foresight of nuns, resulted in their accumulating "riches" in the midst of the workers.

The second obstacle is the isolation of the priest. One of the characteristics of the proletariat, as we have seen, is that they do not mingle with other classes: the priests live neither in the working-class flats nor in cheap lodgings, and their contacts with their clients are of a purely "professional" nature, quite different from that state of affairs still existing in the villages, where everyone knows everyone else, where they are always meeting and hailing one another familiarly.

Consequently, the priest is no longer aware of what goes on around him. Even when one lives in the most thorough-going intimacy with the workers and their families, in the same courtyard or the same block of huts, there are so many little details of personal history which are confided only by slow degrees: So-and-so has a big lad of twenty working in another district; someone else used to run a business . . . insignificant little facts, maybe, but that is exactly why one feels so proud to be told about them.

The priest—this alien in the neighbourhood—it often seems as if his horizon is blocked by the handful of Christian families which surround him and people the desert landscape of the Church.

It will be said that the J.O.C., the working-class movements, have their chaplains, and this is true; but in the first place, these chaplains are strictly confined to the spiritual— to the private influence of the priest on the militant; in the second place, even if they wished to take active part in the militant section of the movement, they would be in difficulties, since—save in exceptional cases—they are not practically, concretely caught up in the web of the workers' daily existence, the battle for a living. They have not, through their services and battles fought side by side with the working-class, earned the right to call themselves representatives of this class. Many priests have as much right as anyone to call themselves members of the French community, since they have won their *croix de guerre* at the cost of their blood, or endured imprisonment; but they have a further task: they must win the right to a *communauté de destin* with the masses.

Less than ever, of course, would this mean a diminution of their priestly character: in some faint imitation of God Himself, they will be separate and inaccessible, and yet immanent to the actions of all. The priest must be a man apart—*segregatus a peccatis*—yes, but not, as he is today, a man isolated from his fellows. This is all-important.

In their childhood, certain priests have known what it was to go barefoot and to have their heads smacked. But they often seem to forget. The people sense this, and they say: "Oh well, what can you expect? They shut them up when they're about ten, stuff 'em with books, turn them into walking brains, and that's the finish of them."

They find they have forgotten how to talk the language of the workers; nor is it a question of using "bad words" (although many of these have lost all their unsavoury significance in these milieux)—but words the people understand, "the words which aren't in the dictionary", as one good fellow put it—the kind, after all, which Jesus Himself made use of in the Gospel. "The priest is like the welfare assistant—he gives a heap of explanations and when he's finished you haven't understood a word."

One is forcibly reminded of a passage in Agnès de la Gorce's life of Wesley. Describing the period when the Anglican Church was feeling the first effects of what might be called the manufacturing fever (the birth of the proletariat), she writes:

"The poor, suffocating in their garrets, are weary of going into the spacious cathedrals built for the consolation of their forebears, where there is no longer anything for them. Ashamed of their rags, intimidated by the proximity of the fashionable and wealthy, they have tried vainly to understand what the minister, perched behind his reading-desk, is saying: fine phrases, caressing the somnolence of the gentry who sit dozing, snuff-boxes in hand. Sailors, stevedores, soldiers, how much could they grasp of this impeccable language moulded in gothic universities, so different from their own daily speech? Despondent, they left and did not return. Unlike the young man in the Gospel who turned away from Christ because he had great possessions, they forsook the churches because of their ignorance and poverty.

"Deprived of their sermon—one of the sole foods still offered to their religious hunger—that insatiable religious hunger of the English people—they abandoned themselves to their worst instincts, drowning their thirst in gin, practising highway robbery, or, totally demoralised by want, dragging their wives around the markets at the end of a rope, like a beast, crying: 'Who wants my wife—my wife for fifteen shillings. . . .'

"But the uneasiness pursued them in their downfall, a kind of mute longing for repentance. These poor wretches would certainly belong to anyone who accepted the offering of their tears."

True, the priest cannot be in every family at every moment of the day. But at each moment he must be capable of vibrating in sympathy with every emotion of the common people.

True again, the priest cannot live in every courtyard at once, in all the sub-divisions of his parish, in each sordid alley. But let him go and live in one of the poorest, in the worst part of his district, and immediately a great barrier crumbles: by the mere fact that people get to know him personally before they see him act, many prejudices disappear.

To be sure, the priest is a consecrated man, and as such a certain mystery hovers about him; but today the mystery that surrounds the priest is false. It proceeds from the fact that many priests, even the impeccable, build the walls of their private lives too high. Now, unless one lives entirely in the people's milieu, it is almost impossible to transform the mystery into light:

"Just look how he lives, how he manages for clothes and everything—don't imagine that that food falls from heaven, all ready-cooked. See—it's the same for him as everyone else. . . ."

How can you go on hating a man who lives right under your eyes—when you pass him on the same staircase, when you hear him switch off his light a little later in the evening, when his alarum rings a little earlier in the morning than the other neighbours'?

When the priest has forsaken the lonely presbytery, when he shares, instead, a common life with the working-class milieu, to the extent of taking a hand in some of the commonest daily chores, he forthwith becomes accessible to everyone.

"He's not stuck-up, not scared of getting his hands dirty—he's not ashamed of living like us. . . ." Ah, if only we realised all the silent desolation and reproach contained in that further definition of a priest: "The man with white hands."

When the priest has got down among the people, he will soon be invited to enter their homes as a friend. He knows then that he must, without being timid, always remain very humble. There is no question of shedding his cassock or habit—on the contrary; but these have ceased to be a uniform denoting him to be a man apart, a man who has lost all capacity for affection, a dried-up insensible being.

It is then that trust begins to grow, that great recompense of the man who has given himself unreservedly to the common people. For him, the people's love and trust are not stinted, for the people love to love.

But the thing which they demand in return, and demand ruthlessly, is love. The present separation between priest and people is a gulf that a thousand bridges will not suffice to span without love.

Nor can this love be merely academic. When a man loves, he shows it, and the proof here must be the fact of living together, experiencing the same joys and the same sorrows throughout all the vicissitudes of daily life.

Ultimately it is the heart that matters, but the heart must educate itself, hold its classes and studies in the very midst of the common people: and it is here that it must always beat.

In this way, the whole practical attitude of the priest will be modified; then, indeed, the last shall be first.

Here is the testimony of a working-class girl militant:

"There is a need for more human kindness in our catechism classes. Because I was worse-dressed than my companions, the priest treated my shabby little person as beneath notice. It was always the smart-looking ones who recited the catechism. I used to say to myself, 'Perhaps he'll ask me next?'—goodness knows, it was all at my fingertips. But the question never came.

"On First Communion day, everyone who gave twenty-five francs had a candle and an artificial bouquet into the bargain. Those who gave fifteen had the candle only. There were three of us in the back row—without a bouquet.

"The next day I saw all my companions hand an envelope to the curate containing a small sum—the 'acknowledgment'. Having nothing but two sous, I couldn't give him those! I daren't write thank you on a bit of paper. So when the priest appeared, I went up to him to thank him with all my soul. I held out my hand—'All right, all right!' he said without a flicker of kindness, without taking my hand. He hadn't troubled to read my heart.

"You don't win children by giving them sweets, but by giving them your heart. Ah, how much more loving the priest should be!

"One day," she continues, "I brought a priest into a poor hovel full of animals, vermin, filth . . . As he entered, he made a motion of disgust and raised the hem of his cassock so high that the calves of his legs were visible. The sick man saw what it meant: 'You've brought me someone who doesn't care for me,' he said.

"There was another priest later. He, on the contrary, lived on a par with the poorest in his poor parish. Everyone said, 'If all priests were like him, you'd be able to see God through them'. There were some poor colliers who went to his church and who, filthy as they were, used to remain standing at the back. One day, he approached them, offered them chairs, made them come forward a little. And next time he passed through their neighbourhood, one of the men said to him, 'Ah! I know you well, it was you who gave me the chair!'"

Fundamentally, what the people ask of the Church is the Gospel, and of the priest a life lived according to the Gospel. When they go to church, they see any amount of candles, statues, vestments, ceremonies—but what of the Gospel, where is that to be found? The Gospel is love, and Love is no longer loved, no longer valued. The proletarian masses do not want us to come among them out of curiosity or for the getting or giving of money; if they have a horror of the word charity, they have a thirst for the thing itself—for charity, which is no ordinary charity, but love accompanied by great reverence for the one loved. Isn't this the whole tragedy of paternalism, whether it come from the employer or the priest, that it claims to be founded on love but forgets to accord this preliminary and indispensable reverence?

"Little children, let us not love in word nor in tongue but in deed and in truth . . . The Father desires true worshippers in spirit and in truth. . . ."

In spiritu et veritate, that is, with tenacity of soul and sincerity of heart. We cannot remain indifferent before the common people; men die just as surely of hunger in certain districts of our towns as they would in the middle of the Sahara; they are as completely ignorant of Christ and His Church here as in the remotest regions of the mission lands. Furthermore, their view of reality is blocked; a wall separates

Christians and non-Christians, priests and faithful, rich and poor, intellectuals and manual workers, bourgeois and proletarian.

So a fundamental renewal is needed of human and *naturally supernatural* contacts; what we need is not administrative feats or imposing edifices, but action which will permit the charity of Christ to penetrate into lives darker than the slums which conceal them. For that, there is one basic, all-important condition: that we live with these people as missionaries, sharing their common lot with all that that involves: identical material conditions, inter-dependent fortunes, the being happy and miserable together.

The proletarian masses must rediscover the priest first and foremost as a friend, a Christian who loves them without reserve because he has become little like themselves, who loves them with the pure love of Christ, with that freshness and simplicity which the Lord Jesus Himself would wish, and which so impregnate the Catholic epistles. Let them sense that there is something else about him, a sacerdotal character which sets him apart, perhaps, yet does not isolate him; let them find in him a defender against injustice, a helping hand when the burden of daily life becomes too heavy— someone, to put it simply, whom they can unfailingly count on.

Will this close conjunction of the civilising and apostolic rôle in the priest bear fruit? Experience alone will enable us to judge. It is likely that it will result both in shy, unexpected friendships and in lively opposition. But would not that be a favourable sign?

CHAPTER VIII

Integral Missionary Apostolate

LIKE AN explorer who stops in his journey to check his progress on the map, it seems a good idea at this point to take our bearings.

The missionary apostolate is not the offspring of a preconceived idea; rather it has tried to provide an answer to the practical needs of the men, the families, the milieux with which it found itself faced.

At the outset, an enquiry reveals and analyses the inhuman and oppressive character of the contemporary economic scene. At the same time, it discloses all the overlappings and inter-relations which exist among the various economic, domestic, social and religious factors—in a word, the unity of man in the complexity of modern society. Man cannot be understood, still less healed, unless he be taken as a whole.

From this comes the first unshakable conclusion: unless the economic machinery is changed, every attempt on the part of its victims to escape its oppression is useless.

The paganising of contemporary society is proceeding much more rapidly than its Christianising. We must join battle for God on this temporal front.

It is not only the people who have ceased to be Christian, but also—and this is far more serious—the things around them, the institutions, the contexts of daily life. Those who grow up in these environments, even when they seem to have retained some religious practices, are thoroughly impregnated with paganism and anti-humanism, like a traveller whose clothes are soaked through with mist.

One of the first tasks, and one of those which, in the eyes of the Popes, seem the most urgent, is the reform of the institutions and general structure of economic life. To change the economic machinery, to overthrow its pseudo-laws, to fight, both on the national and international plane, for a just society, at the same time avoiding the danger of setting up the practical, concrete modifications necessary for this as fixed models for all time—this is the first battlefront. It calls for great skill; to be a saint is not enough—we must be sociologists, economists, historians, philosophers, not to mention the fields of politics and art.

The battle will commence around questions of wages, unionism, commerce and trade, administrative organisation, town planning. To win the battle—the battle which will mark the decisive victory of the devil or Christ—we need enlightened, fervent Christians, convinced of the necessity of their task.

"Let no member of the clergy," wrote Benedict XV in 1920 (and still more, we might add, does this apply to the laity), "suppose that such action is foreign to the priestly ministry because it impinges on the sphere of economics: it is enough that in this sphere the salvation of souls is in peril."

Pius XI later added, "It is not rash to say that the present conditions of social and economic life are such as to create for vast multitudes of souls very serious obstacles in the pursuit of the one thing necessary: their eternal salvation."

With Pius XII, the will of the Church in this economico-social field stands out with ever-increasing clarity: the Message of Pentecost, 1943, is the Charter of this apostolate, and it would be well to repeat here at least the first and last paragraphs:

"On whether or not a given form of society conforms to Divine laws, depends the good or evil of souls, i.e. the question of whether men, who are all called to be vivified by the grace of Christ, shall breathe in the terrestrial settings of their lives the healthy and life-giving air of truth and the moral virtues, or the deadly and often mortal atmosphere of error and depravity.

"Confronted by such considerations and probabilities, how could the Church, so loving a mother, so anxious for the welfare of her sons, permit herself to remain indifferent to the dangers which threaten them, to be silent or to behave as if she neither saw nor understood the social conditions which, whether men intend it or not, render Christian conduct difficult if not virtually impossible?

"This would be to deny that sense of joint mutual responsibility which has persistently animated the soul of the Church for two thousand years, that sense which has urged—and still urges—souls to the heroic charity of the farming monks, the slave-liberators, the healers of the sick, ambassadors of the Faith, of civilisation and science to every generation and every people, striving to create social conditions whose sole value lies in their making open and accessible to all a life worthy of the man and the Christian.

"Never be satisfied in your hearts with a general standard of mediocrity in social conditions, such that the majority of men are unable—save by the exercise of heroic virtue—to observe the Divine commandments, which are always and on all occasions inviolable."

Thus, the call to a missionary apostolate in the spheres of economics and trade, first suggested by experience and the submission to observed facts, finds its confirmation, or more accurately its verification, in the command of the Church.

What joy, what feelings of pride and assurance, to hear the Church in France likewise declare, in the person of Cardinal Saliège, her recognition that no praise is too great for all those Christians engaged in Catholic Action. That this is one of her noblest messages is evidenced in the perfection of its style, the clarity of its thought, the intensity of its conviction:

"The pressure of social conditions is an undeniable fact. No one escapes it. The time of Robinson Crusoe is past.

"To modify the social pressure, control it, render it favourable to the flowering of the Christian life, to create by its means a climate, an atmosphere in which man can develop his human qualities and lead a genuinely human life, in which the Christian can breathe freely without ceasing to be a Christian—this, if I am not mistaken, is the goal of Catholic Action.

"We must constantly have this goal before our eyes, for it must determine the choice and handling of our methods.

"Can the social pressure be changed without changing the elements which comprise it, human beings, that is, composed of body and soul?

"In a factory, a shop, an office, in a drawing-room, in a university, in a college, if one gradually raises the mental outlook, if one purifies—not by elimination but by dissociation—the whole milieu concerned, and not just a few individuals, both human and Divine can flourish more freely. It is in the milieu that the true meaning of life is found or rediscovered. . . .

"By incorporating itself in the realities of every day, Catholic Action gains in range, in depth, in effectiveness. It raises the whole mass and not merely a few personalities. . . .

"A Catholic Action confined to the spiritual, to the supernatural, no longer has its feet on the ground.

"We live in the temporal and the material. To forget it is to play into the hands of materialism. Man is spirit and matter. Matter is a creature and a gift of God, and as such is of great value. We live in the temporal; social pressure operates in the temporal; our brain is matter, living certainly, but none the less matter and not spirit, and it too operates in the temporal. We are not angels.

"Catholic Action can only act if it is embodied in temporal institutions, spirit in matter. Through these institutions it creates healthy social climates, controlling the pressure of social conditions. Instead of chance contacts with individuals, it reaches the whole community, or at least a large part of it. . . .

"I do not see how one is to hold aloof from the temporal any more than the soul can refuse to inform the body. Spiritual and material, eternal and temporal conjoined, this is our situation as human beings.

"I have known, and know still, centres of Catholic Action which are sealed off from the outside world: study circles, amicable gatherings where a great deal of hair-splitting goes on, where endless debating of trivialities dissipates the best energies of heart and soul. Such groups run round in circles, so to speak, getting nowhere. They admire themselves and do nothing. They are engaged in a systematic process of self-boredom. They are frightened of the temporal, frightened of losing their balance, they lack pluck, courage, audacity. Naturally, the young people who are worth their salt wander off, depart. Catholic Action will only retain its humanly valuable elements if it concerns itself with human affairs, and hence with the temporal. More than ever, the situation calls for action, not propaganda—propaganda which is often so childish, a mere trifling with words in the face of the profound changes which the world awaits. . . .

"Matter exists, the body exists, society exists. We can dispense with neither matter nor flesh nor society. Would not a disembodied Catholic Action be a denial in practice of those realities in which we live, which form part of us, matter, flesh, society—would it not constitute the sin of angelism?

"By thus becoming incarnate, as it were, Catholic Action stops day-dreaming and enters into the world of reality in all its aspects, social, material, economic and temporal. It acts."[1]

[1] Action catholique incarnée. *Notes de S. Em. le cardinal Saliège*, 7th February 1945.

These ideas are not unfamiliar; nevertheless, we must continually revert to them. Rare are the Christians who put them into practice, and who realise that they can more surely sanctify themselves in this way than by distributing alms or fine speeches. In a democratic society, they are like so many St. Louis, and they can apply to themselves the saying of St. Gregory the Great, that "Good princes widen the road to Heaven, shepherding in the multitudes".

Where can we find such men? Their task is all the harder since it is doubly lonely: first, because of their small number, but also because in the missionary movement they are generally left on one side. The Abbé Godin pleaded for lay missionaries to go forth and preach Christ, but few regard these men as being real missionaries, forerunners of Christ like St. John the Baptist. Catholic Action is often suspicious of them—not officially but in practice—on the grounds that they are too bound up in temporal affairs. Those who dream of the spiritual life and think purely in terms of evangelising regard them as so much dead weight.

And yet it is necessary that at all costs they be supported in their thankless endeavour, that they feel that they are integrally part of a great movement. They have neither the joy of harvesting nor even the joy of sowing. It falls to them to break the fallow land, to do the heavy spade-work. Frequently they have no leisure and no rest; material cares overwhelm them, each day the battle starts afresh. They are a sign of contradiction. At the end of a few years, they feel that their spiritual resources are dried up; they no longer see clearly, and since the victories that they managed to win were attended by so many skirmishes and defeats, they are unable to assess them.

Even when they succeed in maintaining their interior life at a reasonable pitch, at the price of who knows what effort

and fidelity to Grace, they know that still they have done
no more than clear the way, made it easier for men to advance to God.

They have levelled out the rough places, straightened the
corners, but they cannot force men—perpetual prodigal sons
—to rise up from their swine in order to return to their
Father. This is out of their hands.

Comfort, security, domestic elbow-room are indispensable,
but they do not automatically beget happiness nor a radical
improvement in men's welfare. To turn poor proletarians
into rich proletarians, to create a bourgeois worker, would
scarcely be much gain.

Pierre Hamp, in *Moteurs*, describes, in his meticulous
precision-worker's style, a factory, Gnome et Rhône, where
in 1938 the workers were earning high wages. How did they
spend them? "Bets on the races every Sunday, cards every
night, countless drinks, brothels twice a week. . . . You talk
always of paying, never of educating. Can you wonder if
you have your workers going off the rails?"[1]

Humanity deteriorates terribly quickly if education does
not continually, from generation to generation, keep it
above a certain level, raising it towards greatness. The
saying of the Curé d'Ars, "Leave a village without a priest
for ten years and it will worship beasts", is not an epigram:
it is a fact of experience. It is this, too, which gives the
papal encyclicals all their weight and relevance for those
who come back to them after having experienced the exigencies of life and action:

"Two things are particularly necessary: the reform of
social institutions and the reform of conduct. . . ."[2] wrote
Pius XI in 1931. In 1937 the Pope developed his thought:

[1] *Moteurs*, p. 134.   [2] Encycl. Quadragesimo anno, para. 77.

"If you truly love the worker . . . you must attend to both his material and spiritual needs. You must give him material help by striving to have fulfilled on his behalf the dictates not only of commutative but also of social justice, that is to say, by furthering all measures for the improvement of the condition of the proletariat; and you must satisfy his spiritual needs by giving him the help that religion offers, without which he will sink into a materialism that brutalises and degrades."[1]

This religious help is the job of the priests; accordingly, while the battle for God is being waged on the temporal front, we must carry on concurrently the fight to impart the one message capable of freeing man from within.

Do we not feel the poverty of worldly *mystiques* when we see, for example, a man devoured by the thirst for power or money, or tormented with a hunger for sensual pleasures? The grandeur and the urgency of the priest's task has not grown less. We must have priests, but in a pagan society these priests must be missionaries.

They must live the Gospel and Christ in the midst of the masses. It is not their task directly to change the social structure. If they have to introduce certain material reforms in their parish area, this is by no means their primary rôle, which consists first and foremost in living as leaven in the dough of society, announcing the good news, preaching and baptising. To them falls the reform of conduct through religious education and the refining effects of the sacraments.

Their rôle presupposes that certain obstacles to the Christian life have been removed at the outset by the missionaries of social reform. But their province is neither nation nor trade nor diocese nor city—it is this little bit of

[1] Letter of Pius XI to the Mexican Episcopate, 28th March 1937.

territory to which, day and night, they owe all their attention. Their great concern is personal contact; their great
weapon, personal example. They know that without reform
of conduct, the most ambitious social reforms will be vain,
and sometimes harmful.

In the midst of jealousy and hatred they are the envoys of
love; not of a bleating sentimentalism but of a love figured in
living example. Against the instinctive egoism of others
they try to be self-forgetful, so as wholly to devote themselves
to the needs of those about them. As against the spirit of
gain, they strive to be wholly disinterested, not only on the
material plane but in their priestly office itself—loving the
people not in order to gain more converts but simply for their
own sake, because they are our brothers and because we
carry in our frail hands the treasure of a light whose flame
nothing can extinguish, a water which quenches all thirst.

"I am come to cast fire on earth. And what will I, but
that it be kindled?"

These missionary priests will be at pains to mingle with the
multitude of the faithful like salt—not like the salt that
remains in the cruet, but the salt that is judiciously spinkled
over the whole dish.

They will be a small group united as a working-team within
the parish. Their great work will be gradually to re-form the
inhabitants of the parish area into a spiritual community,
and the church into a centre where this community can meet.
They will not hesitate to say Mass in this courtyard or that
living-room, but it will be the more effectively to draw those
present to the common house of all the faithful.

Perhaps they will have a group of catechumens, but they
will not set up separate coteries. They will realise that they
may first have to convert the more conservative Catholics in
our parishes to this missionary movement, and they will do

so, for it would be folly to try to build Christian communities on the sand represented by our present-day faithful—veritable sand, since each lives his own life without any sense of cohesion with the rest.

When the need arises, their parochial team will be able to split up without losing its identity, so that its members may penetrate more deeply into the various quarters of the parish.

These priests, it is clear, are the servants of the parish community. It is not their task to legislate for the reform of the whole social order: they serve the six or eight thousand persons who live around them; here, they are all things to all men. Their rôle is very great: they are Christ Himself, living, caring, healing, challenging, consoling, teaching, visiting, just as it is Christ Himself Whom they care for, heal, teach, visit. . . .

But the priests cannot do everything in their parishes. Between the lay missionaries of social reform on the one hand, and the missionary priests on the other, will come other missionaries again, and foremost among these the missionaries who, residing in a district, act there on the level of individual, person-to-person contact. The activities of this third group will range widely between the two extremes: in common with the missionaries of social reform, it has the task of overcoming the obstacles to the fulfilment of a human and Christian life, those barricades which blot out the whole sky—but it does it at the most immediate and direct level, in the closest possible contact with those amongst whom it lives.

These district missionaries, single or married, will be those who belong there by birth or profession—doctor, midwife, teacher, social worker, etc. Among them, the permanent residents will play a rôle of the first importance. If it is true that one of the roots of the modern social malady is the

E

absence of intermediary groups between the family on the one side and the city and nation on the other, the most effective remedy is the re-creation of true district communities. The permanent residents, through the duties of their various occupations, constitute the nuclear elements, so to speak, and they can catalyse the efforts of the other missionary residents.

Changing the metaphor, the missionaries of social reform are the field staff who by means of planes and bombs attack strategic points. The residents are the troops who conquer step by step, occupying and mopping up enemy territory. In common with the missionary priests they live the evangelical life, just as they share with them their self-dedication to a specific locality and a specific human group.

As to their regular activities, these will asume sometimes a more social, sometimes a more missionary aspect, according to the needs of the district and the temperaments of the residents; but, in general, their missionary activities and relief work will be primarily educative and civilising, embracing, in a word, everything which can only be directly imparted by person-to-person contact.

Experience shows that these three groups of missionaries must weld themselves into a single mission, into one mystical body. If the missionaries of social reform remain isolated, not only will they wear out their energies but, save by exceptional grace, they will lose touch with supernatural realities. Fighting so far from their spiritual bases, and for the greater part of the time in extended order, they must strengthen their solidarity, first with their brother fighters, but also with the two other missionary groups, who will in turn show them the fruit of their toils and the precious spiritual vitality running through their daily lives.

To the militants of the district, the missionaries of social reform bring not only construction plans for the Christian city, but also the instruments and tools to build it. Their presence, their instruction, above all their actions will prove that the Church is not indifferent to earthly affairs: that Her mission has not lost pace with events, that the fight for justice is not a vain phrase, more especially as this fight for justice will express itself in vigorous local action, and promotion of the common good will be conceived in terms of housing or hygiene or wages or security of employment.

Thus each group will be kept alert by the other: the evangelical missionaries will vibrate, through the missionaries of social reform, to the great wind of the world-wide working-class movement. They will run less risk of slumbering in the routine of the parochial apostolate, while the second group will see at every instant for what and for whom they work.

Without this abiding presence of the supernatural in its more immediate aspects (parish life, sacraments, etc.), without the contrasts with humble everyday life furnished by the residents, the missionaries of social reform would soon risk becoming mere bureaucrats, if not tools of the employers, or else doctrinaires reeling off a string of theories which, originally anchored in reality, have since, by little and little, lost all contact with it.

The checks and retreats of battle will be borne more easily, for each will feel himself supported by all his brothers in his spiritual life, including his own personal rule of life and sanctity. Laymen or priests, we are no longer solitaries, but a community with the invincible strength of the presence of Christ.

The Mission will be an image in miniature of the whole Church, with its lay Christians and Christian priests, with its temporal tasks and its spiritual tasks, with its battles and common hours of prayer, with its common rediscovery of Christ in the Breaking of Bread.

Obviously, this is not in order to separate ourselves from others, to form groups which stand partly aloof from the world of men, but, on the contrary, to enable us all the more effectively to take part in ordinary human life, so that we may bring to it our primary message in all its strength and purity.

I have just quoted Our Lord's words: "I am come to cast fire on earth. And what will I, but that it be kindled?" This fire is charity and the Holy Ghost, but it seems advisable, if we wish to be faithful to Jesus' thought in uttering these words, to leave them their prophetic over-tones: we should not seek to give too precise a meaning either to them or to the mysterious ordeal of the baptism referred to immediately afterwards, this "straitening" on which Christ's work will depend. However, let us try to see some of the implications.

Envoys, messengers of Christ, we in our turn must cast this fire; it is our proper rôle, our special function as Christians, involving much more than the sentimentalism of the self-regarding individualist, for love and unity are inseparable, and it is, as it were, our Christian profession to realise this unity through and in love.

There is clearly no lack of people these days who preach union; but a union through hatred—hatred of this, hatred of that—is one that we do not acknowledge. We know very well, we Christians, that however honourable their intentions, they are wrong; they have not begun to understand the meaning of union, love, fraternity. We know likewise that union does not mean a sinking of differences to the detriment of justice, ceasing to distinguish good from evil.

Now, the general aim of all Christ's work, of His preaching and His action alike, is the restoration of the unity of men, that unity which was shattered by original sin. Through Him, we are to rediscover the fundamental law which—long before Christianity, from the moment of the creation of man—was inscribed in our very being: the unity of human kind.

"God made man in His image. The Divine Image is not one thing in one man, something different in another; it is the same Image in all. The same mysterious participation which causes spirit to be, effects simultaneously the unity of all spirits."[1]

Original sin caused a separation, a breaking up, a disintegration, an atomisation of human kind, a scattering of the flock. "Although God works ceaselessly in the world to bring all things into unity, by this sin, the action of man, the whole of nature was broken into a thousand fragments." And humanity, which should constitute a harmonious whole, where your interests and mine would never be opposed, becomes a swarm of individuals with violently conflicting aims.

The results of original sin have been not only the derangement of man's inner nature, but an ever-gaping wound rending the body of society.

Christ's work is thus seen as the restoration of the unity which was lost—the unity of man with God, yes, but no less the unity of men with each other. Now, it is precisely here that the social rôle, the civic duties of the Christian, must continue the accomplishment in our time of the work of Christ: the earthly task of every one of us, reflecting the Divine Mercy, is to "gather up again from every side the

[1] De Lubac, *Catholicisme*, p. 6.

fragments of our world, to weld them together in the fire of charity and restore to them their broken unity. In this way does God re-create His original creation, re-form what He originally formed."[1]

To impress this truth on our minds, since we cannot here trace its course through the Gospels, let us at least ponder it deeply as it is committed to us by Jesus at the solemn moment when He is about to conclude His teaching:

"And not for them only do I pray, but for them also who through their word shall believe in Me. That they may all be one, as Thou, Father, in Me, and I in Thee; that they also may be one in Us: that the world may believe that Thou hast sent Me. And the glory which Thou hast given Me, I have given to them: that they may be one as We also are one. I in them, and Thou in Me: that they may be made perfect in one: that the world may know that Thou hast sent me and hast loved them, as Thou hast also loved Me."

This, as we are often reminded, is a prayer for the Church, but it is for the Church in its most concrete sense: a Body which comprises each member of the faithful.

Every age expresses itself in its monuments. The only monument which our own has produced is the slum. Among its most characteristic constructions, certain modern prison cells seem to have exhausted the finest genius of its engineers and architects. They are symbols of a civilisation where each man, cut off from his fellows, lives for himself alone. Nor does the likeness end there; it finds its saddest and most striking expression in the modern prison assembly hall—for these model prisons have a room which serves indifferently for theatre, chapel and lecture-hall. Everything is designed

[1] Application to the case in point of a quotation from St. Augustine, cited by P. du Lubac, op. cit.

so that, in an immense amphitheatre, the prisoners—each enclosed in a kind of tiny opera box with an opening no bigger than a man's face—witness whatever is going on without any possibility of communication with their fellow captives.

In our prison theatres, we are symbolically at the heart of our atomised civilisation: hundreds of men and women brought together without any means of contact. It is these false partitions which Christians must steel themselves to surmount. It would be folly and treachery on our part to abandon this task on the pretext that others are engaged on it, for on the day when—yielding to the pressure of all these prisoners—the captive walls burst apart, who, save the true disciples of Christ, can turn this throng of reunited humanity into a community of brothers, possessing the same faith, the same hope, the same baptism?

And so . . . social reform and reform in conduct; reform in conduct made possible by a reformed social structure, and conversely, social improvement made possible by a reformation of conduct. A new organisation of districts and parishes so that once more they become true communities—this is the first and fundamental social reform; reform of conduct through direct day-to-day contact, evangelisation "*coeur à coeur*", conversation "*bouche à oreille*". The Mission must never lose sight of the need for this constant balance, and it is in accomplishing it that it will find its justification, its stability and, if God wills, its crown.

CHAPTER IX

After Three Years

This chapter, it must be remembered, was not written as part of the book. With Père Loew's permission it is added here because of its intrinsic importance and because of the great addition it makes to the documentary value of the book. The three years are the years of his experience as a parish priest.

THE FIRST months of our apostolate were a period of uncertain groping in the dark, of alternating hope and pessimism: sometimes we felt certain that many of the workers still retained their faith—a rudimentary faith, no doubt, but enough to provide a foothold for the real thing—at other times we despaired of even this much.

What is the true situation?

So far, the most valuable result of our attempt to share the daily life of the working masses has been a better appreciation of their level of religious development, thanks to the intimacy and freedom of our relations with them.

"We feel at home with you—you understand the worker."

"You, at any rate, know the seamy side—not like Monsieur R. or Monsieur D. They were a bit too grand for us, we had to mind our p's and q's. . . ."

And we, for our own part, realise that we have picked up words and phrases that enable us to chat away in the colloquial speech the workers use among themselves (although our education here is by no means ended) instead of the uneasy, stilted converse of the first few months.

When I am talking to young people in our *quartier* who are getting married, the moment I mention Angèle le Lapin the discussion becomes animated. Angèle le Lapin is the well-known abortionist. When I speak of abortion in general, they listen with the polite boredom of people resigned to hearing out a sermon. It is this kind of thing which makes us realise how far religion has been replaced by a mere taste for the sensational.

We are convinced that unless one lives in close daily intimacy with the masses, striving to penetrate ever more deeply into their lives, one cannot help building up a false picture of the facts. And this danger threatens not only the religious superiors, whose functions debar them from daily contact with the people, but also many parish priests and lay Christians too, particularly those who never move outside the *milieu* of the practising or would-be Catholic.

When a priest is present, of course, it is the conventional thing to make staunch avowals of one's faith: no one attaches the least importance to it. But compare the solemn declarations which people make at the marriage ceremony and their conversation in the bar, at work, at parties, even the parties which follow religious ceremonies!

Cardinal Suhard defined our civilisation as being characterised not by heresy but by the absence of God. It is a definition which none of us would dispute; but have we, in actual practice, drawn out its implications? Recognising that we are surrounded by a non-Christian people, have we made any radical change in our methods of approaching them? We have improved our methods, yes; but are we squarely facing the demands of a completely new situation?

The Current Mentality

Many, when they talk of the decline of religion, are too apt to think of it simply in terms of the decline of religious practice, e.g. through human respect or because religion has fallen out of fashion; and against this, they argue that the people as a whole still have "Christian instincts". If by "Christian instincts" they mean generosity, fellow-feeling, kindness, unselfishness, well and good; but clearly these are purely natural virtues. If "Christian instincts" means those notes which distinguish a Christian—even a half-hearted or indifferent Christian—from a pagan, we can only say that these notes no longer exist.

The primary truth for a Christian is that "God is a Spirit, and that He has created man in His Image". Now, out of every hundred workers who go down the street between five and seven in the morning on their way to work, ninety-nine have no firm belief either in a Supreme Spiritual Being or in man's possession of an immortal soul. This is a representative figure, as any serious investigation will confirm.

Some—thirty per cent perhaps—maintain with varying degrees of conviction that there is "Something above us" (they never say "Someone"), which they vaguely describe as a mystery of nature: the men usually expostulate if you try to call this something God. These people are not even Deists: they accept an element of mystery in the world, particularly in its origin, and are thus distinguished from the militant rationalists—negligible in number—who contend that everything is or can be explained by science.

It is highly doubtful, in many cases, if there is any conception of a *personal* supernatural Being, although there are many instances again where this mysterious Being is pictured as an extremely intelligent man who existed "in the beginning", who created the world and *who is dead*. The whole question is a mass of confusion.

The usual comment is, "Have *you* ever seen God? O.K., then—you know no more than the rest of us!"

When a woman is anxious to convince the priest that she believes in God, she sees nothing incongruous in arguing: "I always say 'My God!' when anything goes wrong, so I must believe in Him, mustn't I?" (This is quite a common argument.)

"But you say 'My God!' just as others say 'Good Lord!'. One is as meaningless as the other."

The discussion ends in mere verbalism. The very word "God" is applied to anything and everything associated with religion: "My room is full of *bons Dieux*"—in other words, pious pictures and statues.

There are as many gods as there are religions: "You (Christians) talk about your God, the Arabs say the sun is God. . . ."

In any case, whatever people may believe about God, certainly no one ever prays to Him. Religion, they maintain, means doing good. Down in the hold of a ship, as we unloaded coal together, a French docker was greatly struck to learn that I was a priest. He talked to me about religion:

"The Church shouldn't meddle with politics—God is just another word for doing good."

But, as we shall see, even those who flatter themselves on retaining some religious faith have, in reality, nothing but a set of vague superstitions. At best, God is a Being to Whom they pray for health or a job or a win in the National Lottery, and the moment misfortune overtakes them, what faith they have vanishes. Many, it seems, lost their faith during the war:

"If there were a God, the war couldn't have happened—there wouldn't be all this suffering. . . ."

Sometimes we ask the children during catechism: "Have you ever heard people say that God doesn't exist?" Every hand goes up. "Why?" "Because no one's ever seen Him!" "Because He would have stopped the war!" "Because He wouldn't have allowed so much suffering!"

Then those of us who have the children's confidence will ask them in Confession, "Has it come to this, then—that you don't believe what the priest says any more?"

This is no question to put to a child who lives in a genuinely Christian family atmosphere. You needn't discuss doubts with someone who has none. But we have no illusions; we are lucky when all we have to deal with are doubts! I discovered that my best catechism pupil, all the time she was preparing for her First Communion, was conducting an active anti-religious campaign in the school. She was a little girl of ten, unusually intelligent and responsive, with, I suppose, the kind of double sincerity which you often see in children. But as soon as she was out of the catechism class the influence of the family environment resumed its sway and she became a militant anti-religionist.

But the true situation is best seen by looking at its negative side: *no non-practising family believes in the immortality of the soul.*

"Once you're in the coffin, that's the end of you—no one's ever come back."

"Poor old so-and-so, rotting away in the earth. . . ."

"When they transferred my poor brother's body after five years, I had a good look at him—nothing left but the skeleton."

During an informal meeting once, a woman, who had at last admitted that the world couldn't have made itself, exclaimed with an impulsiveness which showed the depth of her conviction, "Yes, Father, but you'll never make me believe that death isn't the end of everything!" And the others present—some of whom came to Mass every Sunday— were silent.

This is the point which must be emphasised: the unanimous scepticism towards everything to do with *spirit*. So widespread is this scepticism that it can infect even the practising Catholic.

I happened to be talking to a worker at the factory the other day—a man of about forty-eight—who claimed to be a practising Christian. His views on life were frankly epicurean, and I was puzzled. He said, "You must get all the fun out of life you can, it's too late once you're dead."

"Oh—so you don't believe in another life after death?"

We were quite alone, so there was no danger of human respect. He told me that he was sure that after death there was nothing. "No one has ever come back from the grave, as they say. . . ." Yet this worker, not content with coming to Mass on Sundays, accompanied his mother to Benediction every evening during the month of Our Lady. I should like to think that he is an unnatural exception, but all the same he witnesses to the power of popular sentiment.

That such a situation can come about is explained by the fact that there exists, side by side with the general disbelief in religion, a widespread attachment to certain one-time religious practices. These practices are no longer inspired by faith, and so in somewhat exceptional cases the complete outward practice of religion can survive a complete loss of faith.

A working-class mother who had just lost a ten-months-old baby told me that she did not for a moment believe in its survival after death. Nevertheless, she wanted a Mass said on the day of burial.

It is common enough, even in practising Christian families, for great grief to blot out the consolation afforded by belief in a future life, but this consolation is always there for those whose faith is really genuine and deep; in fact, it is the only consolation, and Christian mothers will readily admit that nothing else is capable of bringing them any solace.

The rest—in other words, the overwhelming majority— know only one consolation:

"What's the use of fretting? He was fated to die."

They regard the future life as a childish fairy-tale, and most of them think that not even the priests believe in it. As for the custom—particularly dear to the women—of asking for a Mass to be said whenever they "dream of the dead", this is simply superstitious fear which has no more in common with true faith—i.e. faith based on reason—than has any other superstition.

A little two-year-old girl was seriously ill, and her father —one of the workers, a most likeable fellow—stopped me in the street.

"The kiddie's getting worse, they told me to ask you to say a Mass for her. You know how it is, the women get an idea into their heads. . . ."

The phrase points not only to the father's scepticism—for it seems to me that if the women had genuinely possessed the Faith, he would have spoke differently.

In the course of three years, we have met only two non-practising Catholics who believed in the immortality of the soul, both of them women: the first was a spiritualist medium, the second a Theosophist.

To the popular mind, no normal adult person could subscribe to such nonsense. Religion is reserved for children who are still innocent enough to believe in fairy-tales, and old people who need something to occupy them, and the sick, for whom religion, in default of better remedies, acts as a drug.

One mother requested that her little boy be allowed to make his First Communion as soon as he turned ten: "We must do it while there's time, Father—he still thinks Santa Claus comes down the chimney."

Religion is for the nursery. At eleven or twelve the children will have grown out of it. The parents themselves warn us that they must make their First Communion very young, because otherwise: "You know what it's like these days—soon they won't believe in it."

However, religion has its uses: "It's good for the youngsters, scares a bit of respect into them." And by way of compliment: "Besides, in that sodality affair the priest runs for them they won't hear anything they oughtn't."

For these people, the soul and the Absolute do not exist, and even conscience is dead: "After all, I haven't murdered or robbed anyone," they say, meaning "I haven't gone in for robbery like the gangsters you read about"; but to "help yourself" or "pick up" or "walk off with" something, or "to do the same as everyone else", is not, of course, to rob.

There is nothing wrong with lying so long as it hurts no one. These things mustn't be taken too seriously. After all, the priests lie when they say they don't go with women, for everyone knows that's impossible. (Incidentally, priests in general are attacked for being hypocrites in this respect, but people think it quite normal for the individual priest to keep up the pretence: "You have to, naturally——". Conscience, in other words, doesn't come into it, any more than it does when a tradesman insists that his goods are of the best quality.)[1]

Moreover, the slightest excuse for telling a lie constitutes complete justification: to hide the truth from a sick man; to avoid embarrassment; to attain the desired end. And the victim himself would, they say, be the first to thank you. One young woman declared: "It doesn't worry me if my husband deceives me—so long as I don't know about it."

Truthfulness is one of the chief points of divergence between the pagan and Christian outlook. According to the former, there is only one universal law: no one can go against nature. That men "need" women is an almost cosmic necessity which admits of no possible exception, save in cases of sickness or impotence.

One cannot really become heated with the people (at least ninety-nine per cent) who refuse to credit the priest's chastity: it is, in their eyes, so evidently impossible, so patently in conflict with all the facts of experience, that there can be no question of contrary proof.

Similarly with fidelity in marriage: if the wife is absent or ill, everyone agrees that the husband is not being unfaithful to her in going with another woman: "It is pardoned in advance", said one such deputy-wife.

Some young office-girls were discussing the question at work: all took it for granted that their husbands would be unfaithful to them. A Jociste argued with them for a while but finally wearied of flinging herself against a wall of blank incomprehension.

Another thing which betrays the absence of a Christian outlook is the general attitude towards forgiveness. Certainly, people quarrel and make it up again easily enough,

[1] Cf. p.103. A longer experience has convinced Père Loew that the workers have a lower view of priests than he at first thought.

but the goodness and beauty of the plea to "forgive us our trespasses as we forgive those who trespass against us" make no appeal to them.

We realise how misleading notes of this kind can be, and how little conviction they may carry to the reader; each separate conclusion is open to dispute: and yet the fact remains that out of every hundred persons, about thirty admit the possibility of "something above" them; only three or four have any idea of a God worthy of the name; one or two at most adhere to the Credo of our Faith.

I

RELIGIOUS PRACTICE

We have yet to speak of religious practice, which—so far as Baptism, First Communion, Marriage and religious burial are concerned—is much more widespread than the figures just quoted might suggest.

Here again it seems that there are two categories of "Christians": on the one hand, the practising Catholics who regularly assist at Sunday Mass, i.e. the one or two per cent who believe in the Catholic Credo and who constitute the true faithful, and, in addition to these, a few old people who are genuine believers but who, apart from making their Easter Duty each year, do not practise; on the other hand, all those who like to attend the four rites mentioned above, but who haven't even a minimum of faith in the essential truths of religion.

Baptism

A family will come along to "order" a baptism; neither parents nor godparents believe in original sin or in a

Redeemer, while as for the Church and the priests—well, that subject is best left alone. But everyone wants the baby baptised, otherwise "he'd have missed something", "it might bring bad luck", and anyhow "we've always done it in our family".

They consider that they have a right to this baptism: they come and order a ceremony in the Church just as they go into a store and order a frock or a cake, and whether or not they possess the Faith is no concern of the priest, any more than what they do with the frock or in whose company they eat the cake is any concern of the tailor or caterer.

Baptism is often desired simply for the sake of some future end: "I'm going to have my baby baptised so that there won't be any trouble later if he wants to be married in church."

One of us called on a family before a prospective baptism; there were three children already, and it was the newly-arrived fourth who was to be baptised. They all greeted the priest warmly. He explained that baptism presupposes that the child will be brought up a Christian.

"Is that so!" said the father. "Well, I'm promising nothing—nothing at all!"

The conversation continued. Père Georges, trying to show that baptism is not something which, once it has taken place, can henceforth be forgotten, chanced on an unlucky phrase:

"You're not obliged to baptise the child, but if you do, you bind yourself to a promise. The Pope himself couldn't tell you otherwise."

"To blazes with the Pope! I tell you I'm promising nothing—the kid can darn well be christened at the *Mairie*."

And then the mother (who can usually get her own way if she wants) tried conciliation, anxious that the priest shouldn't carry away a bad impression of her family.

"After all, Father, it takes all sorts to make a world—we'll have three children christened in church and one at the *Mairie*, that'll make a bit of variety!"

Not all our pre-baptismal visits are as lively as this, but this was simply an instance of anger bringing to the surface a feeling which is well-nigh universal—a feeling not far from hatred.

One of our militants reported a conversation she had with a mother who wished to have her baby baptised:

"'I want to do my duty by my little one; it won't cost me anything, and after that I needn't worry about that side of things any more.'

"I tried to show her that just as a mother must worry about feeding milk to the baby she has given life to, if she doesn't want it to die, similarly when she has had it baptised—i.e. given it supernatural life—she must worry about feeding it with religious truth; that since the baby neither would nor could obtain this food by itself, responsibility rests with the father and mother.

"There was a painful pause. Then the father said: 'You're quite right. In the Party, we want to arrange things so that men like me do the active work and support the rest'; and, turning to his wife, 'Go and find the priest, and ask him if he'll baptise the baby. Tell him I can't do anything about it because I don't believe in it. But you can—your mother says a lot of prayers, so you can teach them to the kid as Mademoiselle M——says.'"

There was another baptism which we shall not easily forget: the father could not be interviewed before the ceremony because he was never at home, and even on the day itself his job—according to the mother—called him to Valence.

After High Mass, the child arrived in the sole company of the two godparents. And then, just as we began the ceremony, in came father! It was clear why he had been reported absent: at eleven-thirty in the morning he was already hopelessly drunk, and correspondingly eager to speak his mind:

"Hi! Father! You don't believe all this stuff, a big feller like you? Well, anyhow, I don't—see? Still, I guess it's your job." He fumbled in his pocket and brought out a couple of tattered ten-franc notes. "Here—they're yours! You do the baptising, I do the paying. . . ."

He continued his monologue, while the godparents—who obviously believed no more than he did, but who at any rate were sober—wondered desperately if the baby would still be baptised. And so to redeem matters, they vied with each other in suave deference, replying "Yes, Monsieur le Curé," to all the questions in their best society accent.

"Let us pray. Almighty and Eternal God. . . ."

"Yes, Monsieur le Curé."

Our pre-baptismal visits are often a great success from the point of view of making friendly family contacts and getting to know people better, and they sometimes issue in very dear personal friendships: but we never seem to meet with or evoke any specifically *Christian* response.

Against this, we are told that "Formerly the Communists did not have their children baptised and now they do— therefore there has been progress."

This is based on a complete misapprehension. Formerly, the Communists were a little group of militants; nowadays, the policy of the outstretched hand enables people to join the Communist Party and at the same time retain certain of their religious customs. But the active nucleus of the Party is still as far removed from religion as ever.

"I had my last children baptised and it's brought them luck; they haven't been ill once. Why should anyone want to do their kids out of a bit of extra protection against fate?"

First Communion

A working-class mother, surrounded in the middle of the street by a group of mothers like herself, declared—with the full approval of her audience—"This First Communion business makes me wild. Why all the fuss about 'preparation'? I want my kid to make his Communion for the look of the thing, that's all."

"I don't believe in it myself," said a father. "I guess my son will be the same. But my wife's parents and mine would gloom about it for the rest of their days if the nipper didn't 'make his Communion'."

A tradesman declared—*à propos* of his small boy coming to catechism class—"I'll tell you what my faith is, Father—I believe in business. A baker can't be at the mill and in the kitchen at one and the same time, can he? No, and my boy can't be in church and in the shop at the same time."

One wonders how the Faith could possibly thrive in an environment like this!

It is a rare father who accompanies the little First Communicant to the church: and when he does come, he fills in the time playing imaginary bowls. Consider in all seriousness what his First Communion can possibly mean for the child: a nursery event, the occasion of a grand get-together of the family, for whom the religious side of the affair is mere childish make-believe.

"Receiving the Host," said one mother, "is over in a moment. But I'm going to have such a party for my little one when the day comes that she'll remember it all her life!"

One day we had a number of children making their First Communion; an hour before the ceremony we saw a young lad come into the church with five women, all in their best array: the usual spectacle of the communicant accompanied by his mother, godmother and aunts. We had never seen the child at catechism, so one of us went up to the mother:

"Is there something I could do for you?"

"Why, we're here for the child's First Communion."

"But he hasn't ever been to catechism."

"What? Oh, but surely! He told me he came every Thursday."

"And what about the retreat?"

And so one by one the lies were exposed—although it seemed highly improbable that the mother could have been entirely unaware of what was going on.

She made a scene, then became very charming, her object being to persuade us in spite of everything to let the child make his First Communion with the others in a few minutes' time.

"He (the father) would kill him if he found out!" But we remained adamant and the little group went home. Nothing was said to the father, and the feast took place as if all had gone according to plan.

Marriage

We made a point of having several interviews with our *fiancés* before their marriage. Some were frank and helpful and the interviews passed off pleasantly; others made things difficult by becoming restive and demanding why there should be so much fuss about getting married: "At other places, they just take a look at you and ask you what sort of wedding you can afford—everything fixed in one visit."

But however friendly and agreeable these interviews were, they were always characterised by two contradictory attitudes: "We want to marry in the Church—they all do in our family. Besides, we're both believers, even if we don't practise."

"Oh? And what do you believe, exactly?"

They are completely nonplussed:

"Well, we're Catholics like everyone else—we've been baptised and made our Communion and all that—and now we want to get married in the Church."

In point of fact, the young man believes in nothing whatsoever and the girl's faith very likely consists in a superstitious devotion to St. Anthony of Padua.

It is the same with matrimony as with baptism: in spite of everything, people still like being married in the Church: "After all, you never know . . ." and anyway, it's all done in such a rush at the *Mairie*: "You're told to be there at ten twenty-eight or three twelve, and you've scarcely time to sit down before they're half-way through the next marriage. You aren't even given a chance to put on the ring!"

"I know it wasn't very logical of me getting married in church, but then I'm never logical. I did it to be like everyone else—and now I'm having my baby baptised because I promised to when I was married. Well—who cares for logic!"

"I'd prefer to marry in the Church—it's always useful, you know. In any case, my boss won't employ anyone who hasn't been O.K.'d by you."

Confession

No one (so runs the general attitude) wants it—it's an invention of the priests to give them a clear run in their love affairs. ("When a woman goes to confession—well, after all, priests are men!")

Of course, you go if you have to—e.g. to get married. "I'm going to confession tomorrow—I'll just have to tell the priest lies, there's nothing else for it." Ever since we pointed out to the *fiancés* that this is considerably worse than no confession at all, they have practically stopped coming. The following incident is a good illustration of the common attitude. It took place in a ward at the Hospital of the Immaculate Conception, just after Christmas Day. A friend was visiting one of the patients:

"Well, did the celebrations go off all right?"

"I'll say! And just think—the whole ward received Communion."

"No!—and I suppose you all went to confession?"

"Yes, every one of us."

"You too?"

"Sure—why not?"

"And so you told the priest everything, eh?"

"Yes, everything—well, of course, I didn't tell him I have a lover . . . my private affairs are no concern of his!"

Going to confession: a kid's game, amounting to nothing more than telling a priest you've used a few bad words.

Religious Burial

Here again one finds much the same attitude. No one fancies being "buried like a dog"; so the body is brought to the church on its way to the cemetery, in spite of the fact that none of the mourners is capable of reciting so much as an Our Father.

One middle-aged metal-worker went to some trouble to cast an aluminium vase to put on his wife's grave. He had been scandalously unfaithful to her, but, said he, "just the same, it's something to have been together for thirty years".

Although he had never made his First Communion, he saw to it that his wife had a religious burial. He knew she would have wished it.

"Did she believe?" "No—or rather yes and no, like all women." And finally, "No she didn't believe, really, but she would have wanted the priest at her burial." Somewhat like those who know very well that it won't do them much good, but who nevertheless desire an upholstered coffin!

In eighteen months at *la Cabucelle*, we were three times called to a dying person during the night and four or five times by day. It does not occur to people to call the priest while they are alive—his place is to lend importance to the funeral. What precisely, we wonder, is the good of those sick calls we make at the request of the nursing Sisters? To quote one case, the Sister was caring for a man stricken with cerebral paralysis, who remained unconscious from the beginning of his illness to his death. Towards the end, she said to his family, "Since you have tried every means of curing him and nothing has had any effect, why don't you call the priest? He won't charge you anything, and people often recover after he has been."

Following a family conclave, the priest was summoned. . . . Eight hours after the man's death, the wife said, "I did everything possible to save him, I've nothing to reproach myself with. The Sister wanted us to get the priest and we did— but that was a fraud, he died just the same".

All the evidence points to one conclusion: that in this pagan *milieu* (if it is not wholly pagan already, it is very rapidly becoming so), all the rites and practices to which the people cling have no religious value and no connection with religious belief, but are, on the contrary, pure *folklore*. A startling word, perhaps, but peculiarly apt.

In this folklore, everything is on the same level: hearing Mass, receiving Communion, lighting a candle to Notre Dame de la Garde, etc.

"I'm a staunch believer myself. I won't touch food without making the Sign of the Cross over it, and I'd no more dream of squashing a spider after sunset . . . !" This came from a very progressive lady (Secretary of the District Welfare Committee and sole woman delegate to the Federation of District Committees from Marseilles).

A stoker on the docks informed me that he was an unbeliever—he said it quite calmly, without a trace of bravado or ill-feeling. He added that eight years ago, after a serious accident, he lighted a candle to Notre Dame de la Garde.

"You wouldn't do such a thing now?"

"Who knows—perhaps I would. But it would only be like buying a lottery ticket on Friday the 13th, or hanging up a horseshoe for luck—no different!" And it seemed clear that the comparison did, in fact, sum up his feelings perfectly.

Yes—Baptism, Communion, Marriage and Religious Burial have, as we have seen, become the chief items in a ritualistic folklore to be passed on from one generation to the next, actions with an ancestral significance but no reference whatsoever to Christ and His Church.

They are family customs, strong in proportion to the size and solidarity of the family itself. One has "been at a Communion" this year while staying at one's married brother's place; next year, perhaps, it will be "with my sister, the one with the baby". Or perhaps the youngest in the family is expecting a child, and the whole family looks forward to a great foregathering "at the christening".

Thus are the customs perpetuated, family rites associated chiefly with feasts and parties, drinking and dancing. The size of the group which attends the religious ceremony is significant: everyone who can get out of it is at home preparing for the party to follow.

At the afternoon ceremony on First Communion days,

often it is the godmother—"poor thing!"—who has to accompany the child, mother staying at home to attend to more important matters.

It is easy to find and compare three generations of the one family: even if the grandparents are non-practising, they may still be capable of receiving the Last Sacraments with real faith and consolation. But it is not usual.

The parents may—sometimes—have memories of the believing and practising grandparents.

The third generation—the children—do not possess even memories.

We know one family where the eldest girl, aged twenty, was baptised, joined a sodality, made her First Communion and was confirmed—"went through the lot", as they say; her sixteen-year-old sister was baptised and made her First Communion; the boy of twelve has been baptised only; the youngest is not even baptised.

Paganism and folklore—that is how we would sum up the general mentality of the non-practising masses. Our fellow-Christians are often deceived by words, and assume that the Faith still has a firm hold on the people—for them, anyone who says "I am a believer" has the Faith. But all the facts are against them.

Let us add, too, that the tiny minority who practise their religion are rapidly dwindling, and as for "converts"— those who return to the Faith—there virtually are none. Another thing, it is quite common for the children of practising Catholics to cease practising—the boys when they are fourteen or fifteen, the girls when they marry.

There is no enthusiasm among the practising minority, but a great deal of apathy and much in their outlook that is purely pagan (their lives are practically identical with the lives of those around them).

This then, is the sad and ominous outcome of our enquiry, and no doubt it is representative of the situation in every working-class district. It makes unpleasant reading, but it is true. We have a sincere horror of anything that could savour of irreponsible agitation in the interests of a theory. We realise that, were we more holy, we could not write of such things without tears—but that seems to us all the more reason why we dare not close our eyes to the fact that in twenty years' time, even this folklore "faith" will have disappeared—unless we act now. Now we should have on our side the double force of truth and initiative. If we lull ourselves with comfortable lies, the situation will be lost.

For this folklore religion closes people's minds and hearts to the spirit and life of true Christianity. It reduces priests to the level of illusion-mongers, fortune-tellers, quacks and charlatans—nuisances at best, at worst the hated exploiters of the poor.

Remedies Suggested by Experience

We must at all costs have some settled plan, a method of evangelising the masses. Let us be like the king who sits down and reckons his chances before attacking the enemy; if our army is inadequately equipped, then let us defer battle. You can't fight against mechanised troops with bows and arrows—whether we like it or not, this is the age of speed, of lightning warfare.

Since we cannot bring about peace, let us with all possible speed take up our stand and prepare for war. Cardinal Suhard has urged Catholic intellectuals to "think boldly and think fast". We have no time to lose.

In everything I have written so far, I have been careful to avoid theorising and have aimed only at presenting the facts which have been brought home to us in our day-by-day contact with the people. Keeping to this method, I shall try now to report the more favourable side of our findings.

A True Christian Community

What could be better calculated to jolt the masses—this great body of men and women who have lost all hope and faith in God—than the sight of a community of genuine believers?

If fully practising Catholics represent not more than two or three per cent of the population here, they are none the less the largest voluntary group in the community (always excepting the horde of cinema devotees).

It is hopeless attempting to convert the people by argument, i.e. by the intellectual presentation of Christian doctrine. They are not interested in abstract questions, nor do they see the point of individual conversions in a collectivised society. Therefore, it is the whole *milieu* which must be tackled rather than the individual, and the task must be begun not by individuals but by a group which is part of the *milieu* itself.

Although we were able to rouse more interest in the communal aspect of Sunday Mass, we saw clearly that this would result in little more than a merely *liturgical* Christian community—an hour a week was too short, and there were too many rooted habits to overcome. So we did all we could to encourage the evening meetings in which an average of thirty to forty Christians—married folk, young men and girls —chatted together for some three hours about their apostolic efforts and their Faith, ending at 11.30 p.m. with Mass— the culmination of their union with Christ and with each other.

This seems to work well, particularly since it tends to link up the smaller communities in certain other districts to which these Christians belong—true Christians, who realise that they must live their Faith communally, and are responsible for those who live around them. The spirit and dynamic of Catholic Action seem to have especially fruitful possibilities here.

Our Christian community are thus learning that they must live in the world, and not form an aristocratic, self-contained little clique. But they are never allowed to forget that being a Christian means belonging to a clearly defined group—a communion—which is not open to everyone who comes along, and which has its own exigencies and responsibilities: a permanent leaven in society. Christians are effective not in proportion to their numbers but in proportion to their vigour and solidarity. This is almost a truism.

But what happens if we continue to admit to the Sacraments of the Church people who no longer believe in them? The sacred mysteries of our Faith will soon be regarded as mere gestures, devoid of all religious meaning, and for that matter of any meaning at all. Worse still, the salt itself will lose its savour—the true believers will no longer constitute a proper spiritual community, since their most precious common possessions, the Sacraments of their Faith, are distributed to the first unbeliever who comes along.

We feel, therefore, that the creation of a Christian community cannot proceed until there is a return to those rules which govern the administration of the Sacraments in mission areas. Needless to say, we are not thinking of a community which would admit none but the "perfect", but of a community of all who believe in Christ, perfect and imperfect alike: "*Unum corpus, unum baptisma . . .*"

Correlatively, this would involve the creation of a recognised catechumenate for those who are, so to speak, on the way to the Faith, where training in prayer and the explanation of doctrine would have first place.

Suitable Priests

The Christian community being thus at the centre of the mission, what would be the specific rôle of the priest, who is both a member of the community and—in the eyes of the outside world—the standard-bearer and representative of religion?

Now just as the people are of one mind on the subject of God and the immortality of the soul, so are they united in their attitude to the clergy—and considerably less indifferent.

"You're on a good wicket—at seven in the morning (i.e. after Mass) you're finished for the day."

When we visit the sick or call on families:

"Ha, the Reverend Father is taking a little stroll—after all, he must amuse himself somehow!"

"Priests! Lazy devils!"

On one of Père Georges' visits to the sick at Sainte-Marguerite—often made at great personal sacrifice—someone observed: "So you've dropped in for a few minutes to get warm, eh?"

I am not criticising, but simply illustrating a general and deep-seated attitude. People do not believe in the disinterestedness of the priest in the question of money, and consequently do not believe that he really serves an ideal:

"It's all rot, this religion—a lot of tales cooked up by women and priests, though no one believes them really—least of all the priests." There is a striking counter-proof of this: the moment that a priest ceases to depend on the Church for his living, he meets with unanimous approval. "Good for you!" Such, nine times out of ten, is the worker's reaction when he discovers that the comrade who has been working with him all day is his parish priest.

"If all priests did that, in ten years you'd have fifty thousand of us believing in religion."

"Gee! So you bury people for nothing!"

From then on, they talk to you as man to man—they see you no longer as a social parasite but as a militant Christian, to be treated on equal terms, with any member of the Party.

One day, I was down in a hold with a number of other dockers, all of us stripped to the waist unloading oil-cake. At 7.30 p.m., there was a half-hour break for a snack. We rejoined the others on deck, and all—about fifteen of us—squatted down in a circle. Conversation was lively. No one save the foreman knew I was a priest. Someone started on "the swinish exploiters of the people" and "Whiskers", the anarchist from a neighbouring parish, intervened with "I know one—a real swine of a fellow he is too . . . the priest at X . . ." He took off his cap and passed it round in a mock collection, amidst approving laughter.

"The one at Estaque isn't so bad—anyway, he's not too stuck-up to have a drink at the *bistrot*."

I cut into the hubbub:

"Hi, Whiskers! What about the priest at la Cabucelle, do you know him?"

"No!"

"Are you sure?"

"Yes!"

"Well—I'm the priest at la Cabucelle!"

There was a stunned silence and they gathered around me. The first to speak was the Communist trade-union delegate:

"You couldn't be—you're kidding!"

"No—ask the foreman, he knows me well."

"Then you've been chucked out of the Church——"

"No, nothing like that," and I explained how we wanted to earn our living as workers and share some of the sufferings of the poor, just as Christ did. This was greeted with approval and many seemed to be thinking hard. The Communist delegate was still reluctant to admit defeat:

"What about Delay—does he agree to all this?"[1]

"Certainly he does! Otherwise we shouldn't be here."

After that, the victory was complete and someone exclaimed, "Well, if Delay turns up one day to work the winch, I'll be his relief!"

Here are some incidents related by a seminarist who spent two periods working in a Marseilles factory—the first lasting a year, and the second six months:

"One day it was rumoured that there were priests working in the factory; this brought two reactions:

1. You can bet your life they're being paid by the bosses to spy on us.
2. Well, all I can say is if I found a priest working with me in this hell-hole, I'd take off my hat to him.

"This remark is typical: 'I believe in God and Christ, but I've got no time for priests who use Christ for their own profit. If Christ came back He'd be a worker. Let the priests become workers and I might sit up.'

"And here is another comment, this time from a militant Christian: 'The priest is too remote from the worker—and the gulf is getting wider. There's just one solution: the priest-workman!' And he wanted to write to Père Augros to ask him to send me back to the factory when I was ordained—a request, he said, which would be signed by quite a few people, even the non-practising and the non-believers. 'But you'd be crazy to do it!' said someone else. 'You ought to be like the rest of them and get yourself a nice cushy job. And yet, you know, it's a funny thing—if more priests did what you're doing, they'd win the

[1] Monseigneur Delay, Archbishop of Marseilles.

F

workers' respect, in fact it would be the salvation of the working-class.'

"There was great sympathy on the part of the really earnest Catholics:

"'Our priests don't understand us or give us what we're looking for, simply because they've never had any real contact with life. You at least can respond to our needs'. 'It's a great thing that you're doing—after all, if the worker has broken with the Church, it's simply because the Church has joined up with the employers. Priests who are workers like you just can't fail' (i.e. in winning the respect of the working-class)."

In forty-five days' work on the wharves, one of us came to know more men in his district than in eighteen months' visiting, and, what is more, found them already predisposed in his favour. Thus we discovered that far from hindering pastoral work, our jobs on the wharf gave it fresh scope (remember that we are in a mission area).

I am not putting this forward as a general theory or a hard and fast rule, but am simply stating the fruit of our own experience. The form that our plan should take would still have to be settled. Clearly, it would not involve every priest in the area becoming a manual labourer, nor would it mean that the parish should not meet the extra expenses which the priest wouldn't incur if he were simply a worker and nothing else. Nevertheless, it seems to us imperative that we go as far in this direction as we possibly can, if we wish the Church to receive full credit for the experiment.

The point was brought out well in a recent meeting of the local Communist cell; one of the speakers claimed (I don't know with how much authority) that "instead of waiting until forced to work for a living, like the orthodox clergy in the U.S.S.R.", we have got in first, and so gained a big advantage.

There also arises the question of what clothes we should wear. One thing is certain: the cassock is not popular; it is associated with so many calumnies and caricatures, and even, in some cases, with real scandal, that it arouses instinctive repugnance.

"I like you best," people will say to us, "when you're in ordinary worker's clothes." And once we heard someone urging a friend to "Come and see the priest—he's dressed as a man". Both incidents are eloquent.

For the moment, it seems best to let the people see us sometimes with and sometimes without a cassock. They do not, by the way, regard the cassock as any guarantee of the priest's chastity. . . .

Missionary Priests in the Factory

Nowadays, the vital centre of the working-class world is the field of industrial production—the factory. It is here that the worker thinks and talks, and here that he is in contact with political and trades union propaganda. He comes home exhausted, wanting only a few hours' peace, and the little time spent with his family—although it is for this alone that he lives and works—has no determining influence on his development.

It may be objected that the reverse is true: that he brings his domestic worries to work, and that his whole life is governed by his responsibilities as head of the family. That is true enough; but the fact remains that it is at work that he receives what might be termed his culture, and his general outlook and standards of judgment.

Now, the priest is absent from industry. Admittedly, it should be possible for enthusiastic laymen to impress their Christian outlook on their fellow factory-workers. But the record of Catholic Action in this field is sadly deficient.

Militant Christians are practically non-existent in large-scale industrial enterprises. And even if this were not so, could the missionary Church be content to leave these vital formation centres of working-class life without priests?

However, let us return to facts. One of us got a job in a local foundry, and discovered that of the one hundred and forty employees, only one was a practising Catholic—a man of fifty, cut off from the rest by his deafness. The three who stood out as really fine types of worker were all militant members of the Communist Party.

What have been the results of twelve months spent in this *milieu*, both from the priest's point of view and that of the other employees?

"The chief result, [writes Père André] seems to have been the establishment of confidence. Let me illustrate: in a current dispute about wage claims, both I and a seminarist from Lisieux, who had signed on at the same foundry, took up a vigorous stand in defence of the small wage-earner, but one which differed from that adopted by the Communist-dominated C.G.T.[1]

"Our campaign ended, we were sought out by a young employee—a lad of nineteen who had considerable influence among the others: 'I see that it's possible to fight for justice with clean hands. I'd like to join up with you.'

"The identity of the seminarist was revealed (he knew mine already). He then said, 'Teach me to be a Christian. If you leave, I'll have to carry on by myself.'

"We had to present the whole body of Christian doctrine to him, starting out from the ideal of a just society. He became an ardent Jocist. Subsequently elected vice-secretary of the *Section Syndicale* of the C.G.T., during the November strikes he boldly confronted the two thousand delegates to

[1] General Confederation of Labour.

the C.G.T. *Assemblée générale*, declaring his support for the strikers' claims but deploring the political course adopted by the Communists.

"The fact that this young man was elected by his fellow-workers—many of them militant Communists—to the second highest responsible position in the *Syndicat* is symptomatic. During the strikes, when I was busy organising various family assistance measures, a Party militant said to me: 'Show me another priest like you and I'll be converted!'—and, as I burst out laughing, 'No, seriously—I mean it.'

"Here is a conversation I had at work one day with the secretary of the Communist cell. He came up to me: 'It's impossible to discuss anything with Charlot!' (i.e. the young Jocist I have just described).

"'Oh—why?'

"'He'll never admit he can be wrong.'

"'Well, if that's so, he's up the pole—what were you talking about?'

"'The elections. He doesn't want to vote Communist. I told him he was playing into the hands of reactionaries and he just looked blank.'

"'But, my dear Pierre, I can't see myself voting Communist either.'

"'Oh, that's different—you're a priest, you can't.'

"'Do you think I say that because I've been told to? Do you think we get a lot of printed circulars saying "Do this", "Do that"?'

"'No—I know you act according to your conscience. All the same, I bet you'd vote Communist if you weren't a priest.'

"'Well, you're wrong—priest or no, there are two things in the Party I could never accept. I know very well that it's the only working-class party and that's why I feel sad that I can't vote for it, but——'

"'What have you got against us?'

"I explained my views on the 'end and the means' question, and quoted from some articles which had appeared in *Rouge-Midi*. 'We Christians can't accept tactics which brush aside truth and justice. If there were a real workers' party which didn't hold such principles, I'd be happy—I'd vote for it with all my heart.'

"Said Pierre, 'That party doesn't exist—well, make it!'

"'Go on with you, Pierre! You know what people would say about that.'

"'What?'

"'That I'd be splitting the working-class!'

"'True enough—but I'd back you, and there are plenty who think like me.'"

"This conversation seems highly significant. For a responsible member of the Party to commit himself as far as this, clearly something must have impressed him very deeply. Remember that he was a convinced atheist who, unlike his comrade, had no intention of ever becoming anything else. I was able to point out to him in what respects his Party was opposed to the moral principles which he himself upheld—simply because, thanks to a training in theology, I was able to distinguish the essential from the merely accessory. A militant Jocist, a thousand times better than I, might have failed through his inability to make this precise distinction. If he granted too much, Pierre would think he had conceded the whole position; if he granted too little, he would seem anti-working-class.

"What is important about this conversation is the fact that it was with a militant of the present-day workers' movement—of that section of society, in other words, which stands in most urgent need of Christ's Gospel.

"Any attempt to evangelise the industrial worker from the outside is defeated in advance. Attempted from within, it is at least possible.

"Another incident: one Friday evening Charlot and I went to see the foreman, and told him straight out of certain complaints we had against him. He listened to us with apparent interest and goodwill, but the following Monday morning he gave Charlot a week's notice, ostensibly for slipshod work; and told me that if I couldn't work overtime on Saturdays he would have to sack me (this was the first time there had been any mention of my doing Saturday overtime for six months).

"That evening Pierre assembled the men, told them what had happened and asked them to come out on strike—and the following morning saw Charlot back at work, this time, at our request, under another foreman.

"It is worth recording that when the seminarist returned to Lisieux, one of the Communist employees proposed that the Industrial Workers' Committee send him a monthly sum 'to pay for his tobacco'. Incidently, the sole decoration in the committee-room of this predominantly Communist body was the Jocist calendar, which had quite a good sale among the leading Party members. Thanks to young Charlot's efforts, they even bought fifty franc cards from him in aid of the J.O.C. funds.

"I think that we might have done much if we had stayed at the foundry; however, Charlot was called up for military service, and I was forced to find a less physically strenuous job. But I keep in touch with my former comrades, and I am deeply honoured by their continued friendship.

"Not long ago, I was talking to a fine type of lad of twenty-three or so, who is now on the Industrial Workers' Committee. We were discussing the half-dozen seminarists from

Lisieux who were working in one or other of our local factories at the time. He moved me greatly by saying, 'Well—once again, it's a good thing we've got the Church.'

"No one who has not personally experienced the scorn in which the Church is held in the working-class *milieu* could understand the joy which this apparently casual remark gave me. This boy's family is atheist; his father said to me once, 'Your religion is false—still, it's a good thing for children, it keeps them in order, and of course you don't teach them anything harmful. But your ideas were exploded long ago!'

"I hope that before long his son will be a Christian.

"There was an old metal-caster at one factory, an excellent craftsman and a Communist, whose father had received a lay burial and who had himself had no Christian instruction whatever. Yet one day, in front of all his work-mates, he said to me: 'Me, I don't want any priest at my burial—but look here, André, if *you* like to come along—well, it's O.K. with me!'

"And one of the workers present commented, 'You'll be calling for André before you die—what do you bet?'

"I came into contact with several former Jocists at this factory: one of them asked me as we were working together whether a certain thing was a mortal sin, and later remarked, 'One of these days I'll go to confession.'

"It is remarkable how undisguised and general is the sympathy aroused by the priest-workman. Now, when someone tells me that I am 'different from other priests', I can legitimately reply: 'You're mistaken. I have a parish, you can come there on Sunday and watch me say Mass and hear me preach. In my parish I marry people from the factory where I work, and I baptise their children. My parishioners

certainly regard me as a "real" priest, and in their eyes I
truly represent the Church.'

"At present I am in a factory where there is a high per-
centage of women employees. Although their conversations
with the other men are familiar and coarse to a degree, they
invariably call me 'Monsieur André' and never tell lewd
stories in my presence.

"I am bombarded with questions on religion—questions
which are often fantastic, but which at least give me a chance
to get the questioner thinking even if I don't manage to
satisfy him. The day will come when I shall be able to
exercise an almost continuous apostolate which will, I hope,
have great results, and which certainly would be impossible
under any other conditions.

"Here, I don't go out 'visiting' workers who promptly
close up at my approach. On the contrary, they come and
question me."

We believe that it is impossible to exaggerate the importance of the priest-workman in the task of evangelising the
present-day working-class *milieu*. And it seems to us emin-
ently desirable that there should be six or seven of these
priests working in the industrial concerns situated in North
Marseilles between Porte d'Aix and Saint-Antoine.

Uniting Parish and Mission

We are often asked "What results have you obtained?"
We should like to be able to reply with Père Lacordaire: "I
have converted no one, perhaps, but I have converted public
opinion—that is to say, everyone." Here are some anecdotes
which make us hope that such a reply would not be utterly
wide of the truth. Père Robert writes:

"The slum 'squatters' call me familiarly by my first

name, and we are on terms of real affection. This simplicity creates confidence: how many fellows have come to me with their troubles, asked me to solve awkward matrimonial situations or settle quarrels. That could never have happened if I had remained in their eyes Father So-and-so, sitting in his presbytery attired in his cassock.

"Also, I can truthfully claim that at the Refineries I have influenced several militant trades union Communists. In spite of the fact that I didn't belong to their union, they decided that I was sincere and essentially on their side in the workers' struggle—and that sufficed them.

"All the youngsters in the town start work when they are fourteen. Initially, they are no more prepared to become Communists than to become Christians; and when I talk to them from the Christian standpoint about the problems of working-class life, their response is prompt and enthusiastic. The Church would attract them deeply if only more lay Christians and priests were to follow out the implications of their Faith in the social sphere.

"It should be emphasised that all the approval and encouragement which are heaped on us have nothing to do with our individual personalities. What the people appreciate is precisely the fact that, in trying to win them to the Faith, we have thrown in our lot with theirs and become *like* them: like them in our outspoken hatred of capitalist injustice, our love for the humble, in the clothes we wear and the sort of place we live in, right in the heart of a working-class district: it is these and all the other things that we have in common which make it possible for non-Christians and 'ex-Christians' to discover a youthful, fraternal Church in their midst, susceptible of being loved.

"A municipal street-cleaner remarked, in the course of a visit made in connection with the marriage of one of his daughters, 'If a lot more priests were like you—living and working like the rest of us—we'd be much more *in love* with the Church.'

"A fellow I was friendly with at the sugar refineries—an unskilled labourer like myself—said to me, 'You're right to work if you want to get on the good side of us—but with your education you could at least get an office job instead of sweating here at a turbine with nothing on but a pair of pants!'

"But another worker retorted, 'You don't get it—Robert wants to live practically, not theoretically. An office job is a cushy affair. He wants to be up to his ears in sweat and dirt like the rest of us. That's what Christ did—those who follow Him must imitate Him in everything.'

"An employee at the abattoirs declared: 'You dress like us and live in the same kind of digs, and so we all like you. You know the things they say in this town about priests—and yet no one ever has a bad word for you. Believe me—go on the way you're going, and you'll fill your church.'

"And I am, in fact, invited to almost all the baptismal and wedding parties. Each time there are thirty or forty people present, and they have all heard and seen me at the church in my vestments. They begin by celebrating the great event in usual party fashion, but in no time I am on the mat, so to speak—or rather, I am put through an enquiry on our behaviour and way of life. Our principles become the centre of sympathetic general discussion, and it is on these occasions—over the cakes and sandwiches—that our best sermons are preached.

"The other day the bride's father—a sincere and enthusiastic Communist—said to me, 'I haven't set foot inside a church for ten years—not even this new church of yours,

But when you came to see us before the marriage, I realised you were on the right side. You're a Christian and a priest, I'm a Communist: but I say we are brothers. And when you tell me that in my conduct I am a Christian, all I can say is that I'd be a better Christian still if the Church were what you want to make it.'

"When one comes to think of it, surely this covers even the dispositions required for receiving the Sacraments.

"On another occasion I was attacked by a passionately angry mother: I had refused to let her small boy make his First Communion, first because of his own laziness and bad faith, and secondly because of the avowed atheism of his home environment. I saw her again some days later; we chatted on the doorstep, and I managed to make her see my point. Subsequently her husband died, and—as a result of my early severity—she now trusts me and is well on the way to conversion.

"One young couple I knew regarded marriage in the Church as a pure formality. They waited until the eve of the wedding before applying to us, and were refused on grounds of insufficient preparation. The next day they went to the *Mairie*. I saw them several times during the month that followed and one evening I married them. When the little ceremony was over, I told them that they had done well. 'But', I said, 'don't let it rest there. Follow us, together we can accomplish great things.'

"'I think all the more of you for being a bit awkward about my kid's baptism,' a parent remarked. 'It shows that you do at least take it seriously. It would be a good thing if the Church were equally strict with everyone—religion would be the gainer by it.'

"And from another parent, 'I'm sad because you won't let my children make their First Communion, but I admire your earnestness. Most of you let yourselves be pushed around too easily."

One day a woman had a cerebral stroke, following an illness. Her married children were with her at the time, and one of the daughters suggested calling the priest. They put it to the vote, and it was decided—four voices to two—that the priest should not be called. The losers were uneasy: 'It seems hard,' said one. 'Maybe she didn't ask for the priest before it happened, but she was a religious woman, she brought us up decently.'

"'If she were conscious,' the other chimed in, 'she wouldn't mind the priest coming, she's never done any harm to anyone.'

"That evening the son-in-law—one of the four who had vetoed the suggestion of calling the priest—said: 'She's dying—she gave me a good mother for my children, she deserves a priest.'

"The priest was duly called. He prayed over the dying woman, making the others join in, and then stayed a little while talking to them. After the death, one of us visited the family again. The son later confided to a friend, 'They're fine chaps, those priests, they give you some idea of what religion's all about. As a matter of fact, I'm going to go along to their church—it'd be worth it with fellows like that around.'

"Another man, who had refused to go inside the church at his father's funeral, later assisted at a marriage as witness. The priest gave a simple little sermon on love. This young man's sister has just had a baby, and yesterday he sought out the same priest: 'Please let me be godfather—I'd come back to the Church now, gladly. . . .'"

Looking back over the past three years, we are only too well aware of the puniness of our efforts compared with the task confronting us: we do feel, however, that our experience in Marseilles has proved beyond doubt the need there for a *missionary parish*.

I should like to make one last attempt to describe the environment—the mental climate—in which we are working, and perhaps the best way of doing this would be to speak, not of Marseilles and ourselves, but of China and Père Lebbe.

When Père Lebbe arrived in China forty years ago, Catholicism—in spite of centuries of missionary effort and martyrdom—was held in contempt. Why? Because it was a religion of foreign importation, enjoying the protection of the Consulates of China's enemies and exploiters.

The Catholic cathedral raised neo-Gothic spires from the centre of the European concession, which stood out no less incongruously—a stubborn rectilinear *bloc*—in the midst of the round multi-coloured roofs of the town, with its pagodas and palaces. At the entrance to the concession, a notice proclaimed: "*Dogs, Beggars and Chinese Forbidden to Enter Here.*"

Certainly this Catholic religion had its Chinese priests, but always relegated to minor positions, since the European missionaries judged them incapable of administering a diocese. The fact that these French, Belgian and Portuguese missionaries—even the bishops—spoke not a word of Chinese did not even strike them as being a drawback!

Père Lebbe fully realised the futility of buying conversions (for things had reached such an incredible stage of apathy and indifference that it was customary to pay the Chinese Catholics a fixed sum for every convert they managed to gain); and equally he saw that if the Church in China was to be truly Catholic, i.e. the Church for all, it would have to be "Chinesed".

The battle started. He learnt Chinese as well as any mandarin; he dressed like a Chinese; finding that his hair obstinately refused to grow long enough for a plait, he asked his Belgian sister to sacrifice her own long hair (this was before the 1914 war) so that he could braid it onto his.

So much for the externals. But his chief concern was to discover some profound instinct in the Chinese soul on which Christianity could, so to speak, fasten. He found it: it was "active patriotism", the Chinese ardent love of country. But this meant encouraging the Chinese Christian to say to his European co-religionists—as Joan of Arc said to the English—"We like you very much, but in your own country, not ours."

Soon he was in deep disgrace with the consuls; nor were his fellow missionaries much help, for these old priests, however heroic, had remained wholly French or Belgian, resisting all arguments in favour of their becoming naturalised Chinese.

Disgrace was followed by what was, for him, exile: instructions to return to Europe. All this he accepted humbly, but with his views unshaken; and sure enough, it was not long before the very thing which had apparently brought about the ruin of his whole project proved to be its chief cornerstone.

In Belgium, he became friendly with Monseigneur Mercier, who promptly took his cause—which was no less than the cause of China herself—to the great missionary Pope, Pius XI. Père Lebbe was summoned to Rome by telegram. "Can you", said the Pope, "give me a list of Chinese priests who are capable of being bishops?" Père Lebbe wrote some names in pencil, and it was from this list that the first six native bishops were chosen. Thus was the Catholic Church "Chinesed".

When Père Lebbe died, China gave him a national funeral, and hundreds of millions of Chinese mourned his loss.

We, alas, could not learn Chinese in a year—we who, after three years, are still trying to learn to be workers among workers. But we believe with all our heart that here lies the way: that just as the Church is intellectual with the intellectuals, *bourgeoise* with the *bourgeois*, so with the proletariat she should be proletarian. This is not "socialism" or "communism" or "workerism", any more than the love of one's country is necessarily "nationalism".

Now, a "proletarianised" Church in Marseilles, no less than a "Chinesed" Church in China, clearly involves radical changes in the mode of life of the clergy—certainly in their external occupations and perhaps also in their dress. Corresponding to the "active patriotism" of the Chinese is the real affection which exists among so many workers for the people of their own class and district, and their enthusiasm for the working-class movement.

When Père Lebbe advocated the appointment of native bishops for the Church in China, he was appealing to an older tradition of the Church than that represented by the local missionaries—as the Pope's action confirmed.

In humbly submitting to our superiors the question of the Christian community and the Sacraments, we beg them to consider whether there do not exist—in the Gospels, in theology, in tradition and even in Canon Law—more ancient rules applicable to a situation which is entirely new: one where the Church is set in the midst of a fundamentally pagan people with a lively and popular tradition of *Christian* folklore.

Père Loew—Parish Priest

MAISIE WARD

VISITING Marseilles in the spring of 1949 to study Père Loew the sociologist, I made the exciting discovery of Père Loew the Parish Priest.

La Cabucelle is a poor district of suburban Marseilles situated a couple of miles beyond the Porte d'Aix. The parish of St. Trophime is an old one, dating from the period when employers and their families lived in the area and supported the Church and Catholic schools. The Church is surrounded by buildings and courtyards whose use has been greatly altered by the team of priests who are now running the parish. The school, long closed for lack of funds, has become flats for six workmen's families; another home for a young couple has been skilfully made out of the church tower. The club buildings have been totally transformed. A hall is kept for catechism classes and meetings, the catechist and one household are housed in the rest of one club. Three families are in the former presbytery.

The priests themselves live in the second club house. They are a team of four: Père Jacques and Père Max, Dominicans, Père Charles, Jesuit, and Père Georges, a secular priest. The Père André and Père Robert quoted in the last chapter are members of the similar team in the adjoining parish. The accommodation at St. Trophime consists of a fair-sized kitchen, a small slit of a room where one of them sleeps, a larger room almost totally filled by the bookshelves around the walls and the beds of the other three priests. This is all. They have themselves done all this immense work of construction and alteration, buying only the materials. Across the court an old woodshed has been turned into a dwelling for a Spanish gypsy who may be seen cooking her meals in the open, and who often strolls into the priests' kitchen opposite to ask for a bit of paper, or wood, or simply to get warm. They have rigged her up a stove indoors, but as, gypsy fashion, she leaves her door open and lives chiefly outside, she suffers in winter from the cold.

The gypsy is not the only visitor. The door of the priests' kitchen is open day and night. Anyone who likes can stroll in: their telephone is for the use of the neighbourhood. A box is there for payment for the calls—usually made punctually, although I did observe a notice, "Would the tall blonde girl who used the telephone several times on Monday kindly put the call money in the box"! The next day the notice had gone.

The court is of course as much a neighbourhood property as the kitchen and the telephone. One family keeps rabbits there, others do their laundry in two huge tubs, the lavatories are public. A hole has been knocked in the wall so that it may serve as a right of way between two streets, saving a weary walk. A group of older men use one corner as a rough bowling alley. The office where of old the Church accounts were kept has been turned into another dwelling— for a solitary Yugoslavian. As an office it is not greatly needed today, for book-keeping in this modern proletarian parish is of the simplest.

Marseilles, as we have seen, is most definitely one of the "mission areas" described by Abbé Godin. There are now no wealthy families to support the parish in the old fashion. Because, too, it is a *mission* area, the priests have abolished *all* fees (baptism, marriage, funeral), and *all* collections. But they have placed a box for anonymous free-will offerings at the end of the Church and this box is, for an area of such poverty, generously filled.

At the Church door is a notice concerning finance:

> In the eyes of God there are neither poor nor rich. This Church is the home of all, and ceremonies are the same for all and without fee.
>
> But there is no secret source of income. Those who wish to help with the expenses of the parish do so anonymously. We ask you to make no offering *de la main à la main.*

The other source of support for the mission is the salary of one or more of the priests. The whole team believe it to be of tremendous importance that the "Mission" should be integrated into the parish. By working at the docks they emphasise their oneness with the workers, they bring them into a growing understanding of the Church.

Every month the budget of parish expenses is posted at the door.

Père Charles was working when I was there, alternate weeks from 6 a.m. to 12, and from 2 to 8 p.m. Père Jacques had been working recently but was now resting under doctor's orders. He has twice been in a sanatorium with tuberculosis. Père Jacques, by the way, is Père Loew. The letters M.R. in his signature stand for Marie Reginald, his names in religion. But when he became a parish priest he found that the best the parishioners could make of this was to call him "le père original". So he gave it up, and reverting to his baptismal name, became known as Père Jacques. Although the parish is run jointly by the team and they in turn are under the general orders of a priest at the neighbouring Church of Saint Louis appointed by the bishop (also run by a mixed team of Dominicans and seculars),

Père Jacques may be called the leader of this team and the parish priest of St. Trophime.

Born in 1908 and baptised in the Catholic Church, he was educated a Protestant, but soon lost all faith, so that his conversion was from an unbelief that was almost atheism. This helps him in dealing with the dockers and with his neighbours. Like Abbé Michonneau, these priests give much instruction in people's houses, but much also in the church.

As in a medieval church, though in less permanent form, this instruction is begun through pictures on the walls. The priests draw a small design indicating what they want, and this is carried out by a cinema poster artist. Vast cartoons are shaped to fit in the arches against the side wall and are changed with the seasons. I was told of the life-size scene of Bethlehem that was there at Christmas. Now, in one arch were men of every race and colour setting out to work in true brotherhood, and in another the picture of a workman's home, for we were to celebrate Mothers' Day which has become quite an institution in France. Over the altar stands a vast cross made of some translucent material glowing when lit up with a subdued red. The cartoons are not very artistic, but the cross is singularly beautiful. On weekdays Mass is said in the side aisle and the small congregation dialogue it in Latin. On Sunday the nave is used. A portable altar stands in front of the old fixed high altar and on a "big" Sunday this is moved to the side of the Church, and the benches are rearranged so that the congregation is grouped closely around it. The children are put on high in the sanctuary—but at the side of the portable altar; they can see beautifully over the heads of their elders—and if they fidget it does not much matter.

Two priests are in the church throughout the Mass, one

at the altar, the other standing near, leading the dialoguing
of part of the Mass in French, leading the singing of the
hymns, reading Gospel and Epistle in French while they
are being read in Latin at the altar. It may be said that in
one of our over-crowded churches in England or America
where the problem is not so much to get the people in as to
fit them in, where Mass follows Mass as hour follows hour,
such a method would not be possible. Yet even here I have
seen it operate successfully. At Corpus Christi Church, New
York, the people recite more of the Mass in the vernacular
than does the congregation of St. Trophime. Normally the
Leader is a priest, but in case of shortage of priests a lay-
man takes his place. There is also a brief sermon, yet all
are out in good time for the next Mass. However, I am
writing here not of New York but of Marseilles.[1]

Mass is said facing the people. At the Mementos for the
dead and the living they are reminded to pray for all their
loved ones. In a Paris students' church I saw a book in
which people write their petitions to be read at Mass to
"the Christian Community". At St. Trophime that community is small, but a large one is in the making.

Printed cards are on all the seats with the words of the
Mass and the most used hymns. At the first Mass I especially admired the way in which the very few hymns were
introduced so as not for one moment to obscure the central
action. The people recited the Gloria and the Creed, as well
as making the responses. They sang before Mass began and
again after the Communion. At this Mass I was told most
would be believers, and there were many Communions. At
the second Mass far more would be outsiders. There were

---

[1] At St. Trophime the liturgical rule for a dialogue Mass is strictly adhered
to. The congregation recite only " what is said by the server or sung by the
choir."

more hymns for them, there was a Litany of Thanksgiving for our Mothers, and a consecration of them to God. The Litany, the shape of which is based on the ancient liturgies of the Church, especially the Litany of the Saints, was read clearly and very beautifully by the priest-reader, the responses made by the whole congregation. It began with some rather long strophes recalling all that a mother does for her children, to which the responses were a "Thank you" to God for each good gift given through a mother. Then the tempo changed, the thanksgiving became an offering:

Reader: The warmth of our hearth, the peace of our home,
All: We offer you, O Lord.
Reader: The flame of our love, the joy of our union,
All: We offer you O Lord

[*Repeated after each of following lines*]

Our father's toil for our daily bread,
Our mother's care for our happiness,
The family table with all of us sitting around it,
The atmosphere of love in which we take our ease at the
      end of the day,
The night prayers we say on our knees,
The happiness in our home,
We offer you, O Lord.

Then again thanksgiving:

Reader: For the joy in our children's eyes,
All: We thank you O Lord.

[*Repeated after each of following lines*]

For the love in their parents' hearts,
For being in our midst when life is hard,
Because our burdens are not as heavy when you are with
      us,
We thank you, O Lord.

And finally petition:

Reader: All those we love, the big and the small,
All: Guard them O Lord.
       [*Repeated after each of following lines*]
Our parents, that they may be long with us,
The young ones preparing for life,
The couples who plan to marry,
All who truly love and are separated,
All who are far away, thinking of home,
All who are sick and in pain,
Our old people who will soon be coming to you,
That all in our house may be ready to serve you,
That after death Your love may reunite us—GUARD US LORD.

The consecration was made by the mothers alone:

Reader: Christ is now on the altar, in the midst of us. He is there that we may offer the Mass with Him. For you who are mothers, your consecration is your daily life, cleaning and cooking, mending and washing—the unending stream of small things to be done—your days and your nights.
Mothers: O Christ, in you we offer You our daily tasks.
Reader: Your consecration as mothers is to give your life, to give it generously, making no account of sufferings, making no provision for yourselves.
Mothers: O Christ, help us to give ourselves generously.
Reader: Your consecration as mothers is to bend over your children's cradles, hold them in your arms, form them in body and soul and heart, work with Christ to form them.
Mothers: O Christ, help us to bring up our children with you, by you, for you.
Reader: Your consecration as mothers is to have a head full of cares and a heart full of love—to be watchful for everyone's needs—to give without reckoning—to do the most beautiful thing in the world.
Mothers: O Christ, teach us to be good mothers.

Père Jacques preached, and his theme was the greatness of motherhood. The poet, the artist, give us inspiration, and we praise their creative work. But they cannot create life. The mother is greater than poet or artist. God has given to her to bring life into the world, and when she has given bodily life to her child, her work has only begun. She must tend the supernatural life in her child's soul, she must teach it and bring it to God. Most Christian mothers realise this duty while their children are small, but their task is not ended then. Until that big boy has passed the crisis of adolescence, until that girl has learnt what love really means; until she has made her children into men and women, the mother has still a task. It is for the difficult years of growth far more than in early childhood that the mother must prepare, and for which her children most need her.

As we went out of the church, an old custom was happily mingled with what was new. A little picture was given to every mother. But it was not technically a "holy" picture. It portrayed a city block in the depth of night. But in one window a light still showed—for the mother was still working while all slept, toiling for her family.

All through the Catholic revival in France today emphasis is laid on the family. Here there are powerfully supporting elements in French tradition. The family, despite divorce and birth control, the war and all other disintegrating elements, is still far stronger in France than in the Anglo-Saxon countries. And even if the "religious" side of family life is not often based on the supernatural, it is always based on the concrete human realities of family relations: to mourn their dead or feast their living large numbers will come to the Church. Thus on the day after Mothers' Day I joined a family at a funeral Mass. In one way it was sad enough: for early though it was, no one of the mourners received Communion. But what an opportunity for instruction! There were little books at every seat, the reading in French of Epistle and Gospel, the explanations given of the Mass (again said facing the people), above all the sermon, in which most beautifully Père Jacques spoke to them of their dead, of immortality, of their own future beatitude. And I realised the second emphasis of the priests in all this work for pagans: the stress laid on adult education.

In this area is no Catholic school: a catechist is employed, but it is on the Christian parents, together with their own efforts, that the priests chiefly rely to bring up a generation of future Christians. And as Père Loew has told us, one great barrier in this work is the habit in pagan areas of using Christian gestures without the slightest belief in what they mean. One of his first efforts is to make the people face the question of where they stand. The priests insist on having at least nine talks of explanation and instruction with all couples who want a Church marriage. They insist on a promise that baptised children shall be brought up Catholics. Here is one of the leaflets which they distribute:

PLEASE TAKE RELIGION SERIOUSLY

IT IS A MISUSE OF LANGUAGE to give the name Christian to a man who comes to Church three times in his life (baptism, First Communion, marriage), and once when he is dead: merely to be like everybody else.

A CHRISTIAN ISN'T THAT

A CHRISTIAN believes that all does not end at death.

He believes in Jesus Christ, Son of God and Saviour of humanity, without Whom man cannot attain true HAPPINESS.

He believes in the Church, a fraternal community, willed
by Christ.
He believes that men are brothers, and that he must work
for their LIBERATION.
THIS IS NOT WHAT THE WORLD THINKS.

IT IS WHAT CHRISTIANS THINK

IF YOU DON'T SEE THINGS THAT WAY it would be more honest
not to ask for Church ceremonies.
But if you have chosen Christ Jesus, then you should

> (1) Know your religion well
> (2) Live it faithfully, not only to the age of twelve, but
> all your life.

PARENTS	ENGAGED COUPLES
Who want to have your child baptised	Who want to be married in Church

GIVE us warning a month before the baptism, three months
before marriage, even if the date is not fixed.
Don't be surprised or annoyed at our asking you to realise
that religion is serious.
The CHURCH is not a SHOP with people going in and out at
their fancy.

IT IS A FAMILY WHERE THINGS ARE DONE SERIOUSLY

Here is another leaflet:

IT'S UP TO YOU WHAT YOU BELIEVE

Christians have their ideas, non-Christians theirs.
We can respect them all: but don't try to mix them.

Thus, if you think the world didn't make itself, but that God
  had a hand in it, why not touch your hat to God now and
  again?

That's what prayer is.

If you think there's something God can do for your children,
  put them right with Him when they're born.

That's what Baptism is.

If your children want to know Christ better and go along
  with Him, give them the chance to meet Him.

That's what First Communion is.

If you think it isn't easy for two to live together faithfully
  and bear the burden of a family, then let God know when
  you're joining your lives that you want His help.

That's what marriage is.

Many of the leaflets conclude with this notice:

Box for Suggestions

At the end of the Church is a box for those (1) who have
suggestions or criticisms to make, (2) questions to ask on
points of religion. Answers will be given at Mass on the
following Sunday.

The only criticism yet made was formulated by several
women: "We couldn't feed our families so cheaply. The
priests should spend more on housekeeping." And advantage
is increasingly taken of the open door to lay upon the kitchen
table very practical gifts of food. The sum allocated to the
priests' food is indeed a very small one—three thousand
francs per priest per month—i.e. barely three pounds a

month. There is no charge for a housekeeper since they do all their own work. As I came into the court one morning I found Père Max in his habit sweeping out the kitchen. One priest cooks the lunch, another washes up. All is spotlessly clean and the cooking is good enough to make the simple food very agreeable.

I was so much interested by this matter of the budget that I got permission to look through a year's collection, out of which I copied three months' figures. These were months of rather heavy construction work, the materials for which are the biggest item. In normal months the heaviest expenses are the posters, leaflets—printed or stencilled— gramophone records and other means of propaganda (about four thousand francs a month). Each priest draws for his own expenses two thousand francs a month; entertaining costs another one thousand five hundred. But around Christmas, parcels and entertaining rose to twelve thousand five hundred.

Looking over a full year one noticed a biggish deficit on some months, but, said Père Loew, "It is always made up the next month"; and he added with a note of most simple sincerity, "We are never the least worried about money."

As Père Chenu once said: "If a priest keeps his parish alive, his parish will keep him alive." And of the vitality of this parish there can be no doubt.

But to return to Mothers' Day.

One of the most noteworthy things about this parish is the degree to which it has become the centre of the joys and sorrows, the problems and the celebrations of the entire area. Partly the good luck of its spacious courts and numerous buildings, but chiefly the radiance of its lay and clerical teams.

Anyhow, it was in the large court of the old school that

the neighbourhood held its secular celebration of Mothers'
Day. And it was chiefly Mademoiselle Marie from the
Residence and the Jeunes Foyers from the schoolhouse that
had planned and prepared it. It consisted chiefly of a performance by the children for their mothers' enjoyment.
There were some distressing contretemps: the loudspeaker,
after emitting a series of groans, squeaks, and a final roar,
went out of commission: black clouds finally broke in tor-
rential rain, and the actors had to rush into the house and
finish the performance under cover. But neither the break-
down of an instrument, nor the falling of the rain could
damp the good spirits or spoil the enjoyment of the mothers
and their friends. Sitting on benches, rejoicing in the good
looks of their offspring, exchanging witticisms with their
friends, the mothers appeared supremely happy: it was of
course the one audience that amateur actors can delight far
more than could professionals.

The children really were excellent: little southerners with
the good looks and the verve that belong to the Mediterranean coast. They united Italian beauty with French wit
and readiness. Not disconcerted by the failure of the loudspeaker, they put on a fine performance on the exceedingly
narrow stage. Once or twice a child fell off into the audience
and was caught and handed up again, adding greatly to the
general enjoyment. There were recitations, songs, gym-
nastics—these last not especially good, but the mothers
appeared to think highly of them. The high point was a
short play about a wedding feast. The little bride in long
white dress and veil, the bridegroom surrounded by a high
wall of parental collar, the guests tripping over their long
skirts and trousers, were greeted with howls of mirth.

Sitting at the back and with my ear imperfectly attuned to
the accent (and the slang!) I was in worse case than most at

the failure of the loudspeaker. I thought I caught a reference to the fact that all the guests were "lit up". I became certain of it as I watched the small boys rendering their various states—"one over the eight", "half seas over", etc., with the profound delight of the young in acting something that is really easy to act!

Half-way through the performance, two varieties were introduced. Children in the audience, if bringing a mother with them, were invited to partake of cakes and hot chocolate. For a while the benches were cleared; and then came another high spot. The municipality had decided to award a medal to the mother of the largest family in the area. An alderman led the blushing lady onto the stage. Mother of twelve children, she looked amazingly young. The medal was pinned on, a speech was made, and then her husband joined her on the stage and kissed her soundly amid universal applause.

Thinking of this scene I was haunted by an echo: a resemblance? a contrast? Suddenly I remembered. It was the chapter in *Madame Bovary* describing an agricultural show where an old servant receives a silver medal. All the fat cattle have been crowned with laurel and their fatter owners recompensed with gold. And then this poor bent old woman, understanding nothing, her gnarled hands stained from the stables, her wooden shoes, her blue working dress, her body bent by fifty-four years of toil, is pushed and pulled forward to receive the price of her slavery. There is adulation for the prosperous farmers and even for their beasts, but with almost open contempt the medal is bestowed on the shrinking old woman.

The scene epitomises what all the novels of the period indicate: a society already largely without God, in which man has lost contact hopelessly with his fellow-man. Money and class, success or failure have become more important than the main facts concerning any man—his creation by God, his redemption by Christ's blood, his imperishable immortal spirit.

In *Madame Bovary* the Agricultural Show was written up in the newspapers by the local chemist—a free-thinker of some distinction in the neighbourhood. "Nothing untoward", he said, "occurred to mar this family gathering. . . . The only noteworthy fact was the absence of the clergy. Doubtless the sacristy notion of progress is different from ours. Well, that's your own affair, gentlemen of Loyola."

Here in Marseilles too the notion of progress had not been that of the sacristy—where its true ideals had been remembered. Wise were those clergy who marked by their absence the failure of nineteenth-century success. But today the presence of the priests is truly creative—for they are restoring the lost sanities and leading in an effort to restore the idea of Man, and with it faith in God.

And I watched the priests of La Cabucelle. There they were, all moving about, exchanging handshakes with men and women (how the French love shaking hands!), receiving confidences. They were as much at home here in their lay dress as in the morning in their habits and vestments going up to the altar of God and breaking the Bread of Life to their flocks.

And I thought of Abbé Godin and his desire that by an analogy with the Incarnation of Christ, the priest should take to himself the form of the human community, even if that community be pagan, that thereby he may raise it and transmute it. I thought of Père Max sweeping the kitchen, of Père Loew himself eating with his friends food that had come from a garbage pail. And as they moved about each separately, but with a unity of aim and action that was almost visible, I thought of what these teams of priestly action mean, of how four men are in fact *the* parish priest of La Cabucelle.

For what is it, asks Père Loew, to work as a team? It is to share responsibility, to share authority, to work together, to have a spirit of youth that laughs at hardship—and laughs in unison. It is to live together an intense spiritual life that draws the team into an ever-deepening union with the life of God Himself. And here Père Loew finds a daring analogy: so close must be the union, so united the action of a team, that the inner union must be expressed by the shadow of the Divine Mystery of the Trinity. Separate in their persons, all their works *ad extra* must be works of the entire team.

Into the depths of this spiritual unity the visitor can only take a reverent glimpse. But the works *ad extra* may be seen by all, and may lead us to the Source of all work that is worthy of its Divine Author, who is the Reward of His workers.